Level 1 • Part 2
Integrated Chinese
中文聽説讀寫

WORKBOOK Traditional Characters

Third Edition

THIRD EDITION BY

Yuehua Liu and Tao-chung Yao
Nyan-Ping Bi, Yaohua Shi, Liangyan Ge, Yea-fen Chen

ORIGINAL EDITION BY

Tao-chung Yao and Yuehua Liu
Yea-fen Chen, Liangyan Ge, Nyan-Ping Bi,
Xiaojun Wang, Yaohua Shi

CHENG & TSUI COMPANY
Boston

26 25 24 23 22   8 9 10 11 12

Published by
Cheng & Tsui Company, Inc.
25 West Street
Boston, MA 02111-1213 USA
Fax (617) 426-3669
www.cheng-tsui.com
"Bringing Asia to the World"™

ISBN 978-0-88727-675-0

Cover Design: studioradia.com

Cover Photographs: Man with map © Getty Images; Shanghai skyline © David Pedre/iStockphoto; Building with masks © Wu Jie; Night market © Andrew Buko. Used by permission.

Interior Design: Wanda España, Wee Design

Illustrations: 洋洋兔动漫

The *Integrated Chinese* series includes books, workbooks, character workbooks, audio products, multimedia products, teacher's resources, and more. Visit **www.cheng-tsui.com** for more information on the other components of *Integrated Chinese*.

Printed in the United States of America

Contents

Preface to the Third Edition

This new Workbook accompanies the third edition of *Integrated Chinese* (*IC*). In response to teachers' feedback and requests, the new *Integrated Chinese Level 1* includes 20 lessons (10 in Part 1 and 10 in Part 2), instead of 23 lessons as in the earlier editions. The format of the third edition Workbook remains largely unchanged. For maximum flexibility in pacing, each lesson is divided into two parts corresponding to the two sections of the lesson in the textbook. The exercises cover the language form and the four language skills of listening, speaking, reading, and writing.

We have also made several improvements and added new features in the new edition of the Workbook.

Three Modes of Communication Clearly Labeled

We would like to point out that our exercises cover the three modes of communication as explained in "Standards for Foreign Language Learning in the 21st Century": interpretive, interpersonal and presentational. We have labeled the exercises as interpretive, interpersonal or presentational wherever applicable.

More Authentic Materials Incorporated

To build a bridge between the pedagogical materials used in the classroom and the materials that the student will face in the target language environment, we have included authentic materials in the exercises for all lessons.

New Illustrations Added

To make the exercises more interesting and appealing, we have added many illustrations to the exercises. These visual images increase the variety of exercise types, and also stimulate the student to answer questions directly in Chinese without going through the translation process.

Contextualized Grammar Exercises and Task-Oriented Assignments Provided

The ultimate goal of learning any language is to be able to communicate in that language. With that goal in mind, we pay equal attention to language form and language function, and have created task-based exercises to train the student to handle real life situations using the language accurately and appropriately. We have rewritten many items, especially in the translation section, to provide linguistic context and to reflect the language used in real life.

Learner-Centered Tasks Included

We believe that the exercises in the Workbook should not only integrate the materials of the Textbook, but also relate to the student's life. We include exercises that simulate daily life with topics and themes that are relevant and personal to the student. We hope these exercises will actively engage students in the subject matter, and keep them interested in the language learning process. Since the world is constantly changing, we also have tried to add exercises that will train the student to meet the needs of today's world, such as writing e-mail messages in Chinese.

New Rejoinders Added

To help the student develop interpersonal skills, we have added a couple of rejoinders to each lesson. A rejoinder is used to see if the student can answer a question or respond to a remark logically and meaningfully.

New Exercises for Storytelling Added

To train students to describe what they see and use their language skills to construct narratives, we have added one storytelling exercise to each lesson. This exercise will let the student develop skills for organizing ideas and presenting them in a coherent manner. It also provides practice in using transitional elements and cohesive devices to make the story progress smoothly and logically. This exercise is suitable for either speaking or writing. The teacher can ask the student to submit the story as a written exercise and/or ask the student to make an oral presentation in class.

New Review Exercises Supplied

Every five lessons, a cumulative review unit is available to those students who wish to do a periodic progress check. The review units do not introduce any new learning materials, and can be included in or excluded from any curriculum planning, according to individual needs. These units are flexible, short, and useful as a review tool.

We would like to take this opportunity to thank all those who have given us feedback in the past, and extend our sincere gratitude to Professor Zheng-sheng Zhang of San Diego State University for his invaluable editorial comments and to Ms. Laurel Damashek at Cheng & Tsui for her support throughout the production process. We welcome your comments and feedback; please send any observations or suggestions to **editor@cheng-tsui.com.**

Preface to the Second Edition

In designing the Level One workbook exercises for *Integrated Chinese*, we strove to give equal emphasis to the students' listening, speaking, reading and writing skills. There are different difficulty levels in order to provide variety and flexibility to suit different curriculum needs. Teachers should assign the exercises at their discretion; they should not feel pressured into using all of them and should feel free to use them out of sequence, if appropriate. Moreover, teachers can complement this workbook with their own exercises.

The exercises in each lesson are divided into two parts. The exercises in Part One are for the first dialogue and those in Part Two are for the second dialogue. This way, the two dialogues in each lesson can be taught separately. The teacher can use the first two or three days to teach the first dialogue and ask the students to do all the exercises in Part One, then go on to teach the second dialogue. The teacher can also give two separate vocabulary tests for the two dialogues so as to reduce the pressure of memorizing too many new words at the same time.

Listening Comprehension

All too often listening comprehension is sacrificed in a formal classroom setting because of time constraints. Students tend to focus their time and energy on the mastery of a few grammar points. This workbook tries to remedy this imbalance by including a substantial number of listening comprehension exercises. There are two categories of listening exercises; both can be done on the students' own time or in the classroom. In either case, it is important to have the instructor review the students' answers for accuracy.

The first category of listening exercises, which is at the beginning of this section, is based on the text of each lesson. For the exercises to be meaningful, students should *first* study the vocabulary list, and *then* listen to the recordings *before* attempting to read the texts. The questions are provided to help students' aural understanding of the texts and to test their reading comprehension.

The second category of listening exercises consists of an audio CD recording of two or more mini-dialogues or narratives. These exercises are designed to give students extra practice on the vocabulary and grammar points introduced in the lesson. Some of the exercises, especially ones that ask students to choose among several possible answers, are significantly more difficult than others. These exercises should be assigned towards the end of the lesson, when the students have become familiar with the content of the lesson.

Speaking Exercises

Here, too, there are two types of exercises. They are designed for different levels of proficiency within each lesson and should be assigned at the appropriate time.

To help students apply their newly-acquired vocabulary and grammatical understanding to meaningful communication, we first ask them questions related to the dialogues and narratives, and then ask them questions related to their own lives. These questions require a one- or two-sentence answer. By stringing together short questions and answers, students can construct their own mini-dialogues, practice in pairs or take turns asking or answering questions.

Once they have gained some confidence, students can progress to the more difficult questions, where they are invited to express opinions on a number of topics. Typically, these questions are abstract, so they gradually teach students to express their opinions in longer conversations. As the school year progresses, these types of questions should take up more class discussion time. Because this second type of speaking exercise is quite challenging, it should be attempted only *after* students are well grounded in the grammar and vocabulary of a particular lesson. Usually, this occurs *not immediately* after students have completed the first part of the speaking exercises.

Reading Comprehension

The first part of this section of the lesson asks questions based on the dialogues in the textbook. The second part offers several reading passages with questions that are relevant to the themes of the current lesson.

Writing and Grammar Exercises

Grammar and Usage

These drills and exercises are designed to solidify students' grasp of important grammar points. Through brief exchanges, students answer questions using specific grammatical forms, or are given sentences to complete. Because they must provide context for these exercises, students cannot treat them as simple mechanical repetition drills.

Translation

Translation has been a tool for language teaching throughout the ages, and positive student feedback confirms our belief that it continues to play an important role. The exercises we have devised serve to reinforce two primary areas: one, to get students to apply specific grammatical structures; and two, to allow students to build their ever-increasing vocabulary. Ultimately, our hope is that this dual-pronged approach will enable students to understand that it takes more than just literal translation to convey an idea in a foreign language.

Writing Practice

This is the culmination of the written exercises, and it is where students learn to express themselves in writing. Many of the topics overlap with those used in oral practice. We expect that students will find it easier to put in writing what they have already learned to express orally.

LESSON 11   Talking about the Weather

第十一課 談天氣

PART ONE

Dialogue I: Tomorrow's Weather Will Be Even Better!

I. Listening Comprehension

A. Textbook Dialogue (True/False) (INTERPRETIVE)

( ) **1.** Yesterday's weather was very bad.

( ) **2.** Today's weather is better, but still a little cold.

( ) **3.** Gao Xiaoyin knew that her brother had invited Bai Ying'ai to go skating with him but didn't tell him that Bai Ying'ai had gone to New York.

( ) **4.** Gao Xiaoyin seems better informed than her brother about a lot of things.

( ) **5.** Gao Wenzhong will watch ice skating on DVD at home tomorrow.

B. Workbook Dialogue (True/False) (INTERPRETIVE)

( ) **1.** This conversation probably took place in a sporting goods store.

( ) **2.** Bai Ying'ai and Wang Peng went skating together without inviting Li You and Gao Wenzhong.

( ) **3.** Bai Ying'ai skates the best among the four of them.

( ) **4.** Gao Wenzhong will hire a coach for himself and Li You.

( ) **5.** Gao Wenzhong and Li You have decided to go to the park tomorrow.

C. Listening Rejoinder (INTERPERSONAL)

In this section, you will hear two speakers talking. After hearing the first speaker, select the best from the four possible responses given by the second speaker.

_____

II. Speaking Exercises

A. Answer the questions in Chinese based on the Textbook Dialogue. (INTERPRETIVE/PRESENTATIONAL)

1. How was today's weather in comparison with yesterday's?
2. What was Gao Wenzhong's plan for tomorrow?
3. Where did Gao Xiaoyin read the weather forecast?
4. Why did Gao Xiaoyin tell Gao Wenzhong to change his plan?

B. Ask your partner what he/she usually does when the weather is not good. (INTERPERSONAL)

C. Check this weekend's weather forecast. Find out if the weather will be nice or not and describe what you plan to do according to the predicted weather conditions. (INTERPRETIVE/PRESENTATIONAL)

III. Reading Comprehension (INTERPRETIVE)

A. Building Words

If you combine the *huá* in *huá bīng* with the *shuǐ* in *hē shuǐ*, you have *huá shuǐ*, as seen in #1 below. Can you guess what the word *huá shuǐ* means? Complete this section by providing the characters, the *pinyin*, and the English equivalent of each new word formed this way. You may consult a dictionary if necessary.

	new word	*pinyin*	English

1. "滑冰" 的 "滑" + "喝水" 的 "水"

   → 滑+水 → _____ _____ _____

2. "滑冰" 的 "滑" + "下雪" 的 "雪"

   → 滑+雪 → _____ _____ _____

3. "學校" 的 "校" + "公園" 的 "園"

   → 校+園 → _____ _____ _____

4.　"暖和"的"暖"＋"天氣"的"氣"

　→　暖＋氣　→　_____　　_____　　_____

5.　"飛機"的"飛"＋"看碟"的"碟"

　→　飛＋碟　→　_____　　_____　　_____

B. Read the following passage and answer the questions.

　　星期五下午王朋約了李友星期天一起去公園滑冰。可是電視上的天氣預報說，星期天的天氣不好，會下雪。王朋就給李友打電話，告訴她星期天不去公園了。星期天上午王朋請李友來他的宿舍看碟，可是星期天的天氣很好，不但沒下雪，而且很暖和。王朋說："以後電視上說會下雪，我們就可以去公園玩兒。電視上說天氣很好，我們就只能在家看碟了。"

Questions: (True/False)

( )**1.** The story took place in the summer.
( )**2.** They had to change their plan for Sunday because of the weather forecast.
( )**3.** Wang Peng got the weather forecast from the internet.
( )**4.** The forecast predicted that it would snow.
( )**5.** Wang Peng was glad that he and Li You were not out on Sunday.
( )**6.** According to Wang Peng, the weather forecast is not reliable.

C. Read the following passage and answer the questions.

　　現在已經是一月了，可是不但不下雪，而且很暖和。大家都很高興，可是小美不太高興。她問李友："一月的天氣怎麼跟十月一樣啊？什麼時候才會冷啊？"李友不懂小美為什麼希望天氣冷，就去問白英愛，才知道小美上個星期買了一件漂亮的新大衣。

Questions (Multiple Choice)

( ) **1.** The season described in the story is _____.

    a. spring
    b. summer
    c. autumn
    d. winter

( ) **2.** Which of the following best describes the current weather conditions?

    a. seasonably cold
    b. unseasonably warm
    c. seasonably rainy
    d. unseasonably snowy

( ) **3.** To Li You, Xiaomei's comments on the weather were _____.

    a. interesting
    b. annoying
    c. expected
    d. perplexing

( ) **4.** Which of the statements is most likely to be true?

    a. Xiaomei knows both Li You and Bai Ying'ai.
    b. Xiaomei knows Li You but not Bai Ying'ai.
    c. Xiaomei knows neither Li You nor Bai Ying'ai.
    d. Xiaomei knows Bai Ying'ai but not Li You.

( ) **5.** According to Bai Ying'ai, Xiaomei is quite eager to _____.

    a. experience cold weather
    b. experience typical October-like weather
    c. wear her new overcoat
    d. return her new overcoat

D. Answer the following questions based on the authentic material provided.

城市	天氣	氣溫(℃)	城市	天氣	氣溫(℃)
華盛頓		34~24	新德里		35~27
紐約		32~23	德黑蘭		39~25
芝加哥		26~18	莫斯科		26~15
洛杉磯		24~17	聖彼得堡		26~15
舊金山		20~12	伊斯坦布爾		30~21
溫哥華		22~11	雅典		34~25
蒙特利爾		26~16	維也納		27~15
多倫多		28~20	日內瓦		28~12
阿卡波克		24~11	法蘭克福		25~14
巴西利亞		25~13	柏林		21~11
里約熱內盧		26~17	漢堡		20~13
布宜諾斯艾利斯		12~9	巴黎		25~15
聖地亞哥		11~6	里昂		30~18
東京		31~24	曼徹斯特		18~10
曼谷		33~25	倫敦		21~14
新加坡		29~25	斯德哥爾摩		19~12
吉隆坡		30~23	馬德里		37~17
馬尼拉		32~25	巴塞羅那		29~22
惠靈頓		13~9	米蘭		29~18
悉尼		16~8	華沙		23~12
卡拉奇		33~28	開普敦		16~6

紐約這一天的天氣冷還是暖和？

_____

你還知道哪些城市的名字？

_____

IV. Writing Exercises

A. This is how a retailer touts his merchandise:

我們的東西不但好，而且便宜。

Other selling points:

多、新、好看、好用；男人喜歡、女人喜歡；大人喜歡、小孩喜歡

1. _____

2. _____

3. _____

However, his customers think otherwise:

他們的東西不但不好，而且不便宜。

1. _____

2. _____

3. _____

B. Little Wang has become environmentally conscious, and is trying to save energy in any way he can.

EXAMPLE:

→ 小王以前上網聊天兒，現在不上網聊天兒了。

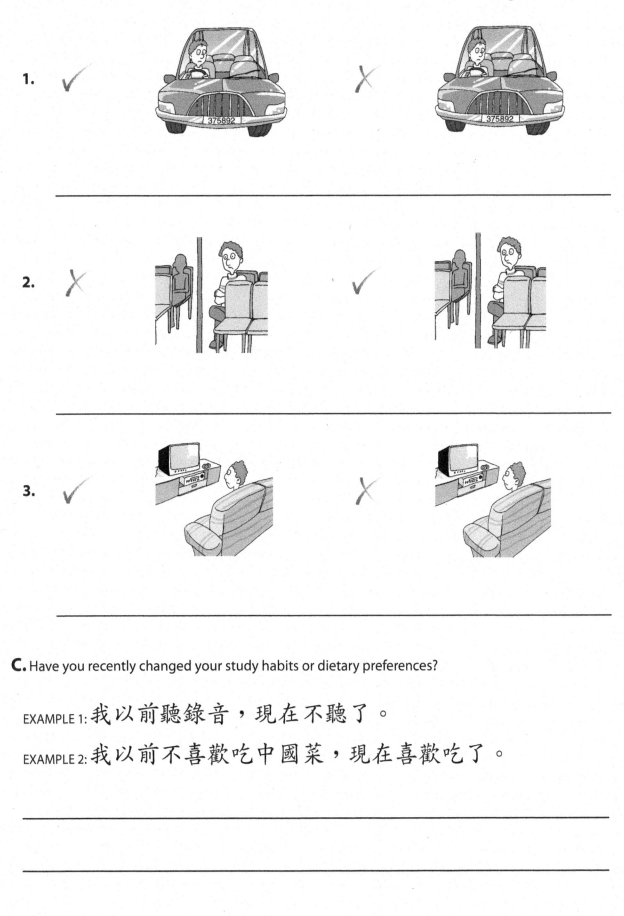

C. Have you recently changed your study habits or dietary preferences?

EXAMPLE 1: 我以前聽錄音，現在不聽了。

EXAMPLE 2: 我以前不喜歡吃中國菜，現在喜歡吃了。

_____

_____

_____

D. Weather Forecast

Here's a weather forecast for New York and Beijing tomorrow. Interpret the forecast to write whether it will snow in each place, and if it will be colder or warmer than the place where you are.

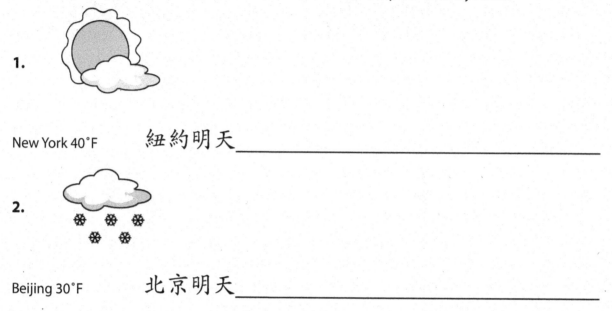

1.

New York 40°F   紐約明天＿＿＿＿＿＿＿＿＿＿＿＿＿＿＿＿＿＿

2.

Beijing 30°F   北京明天＿＿＿＿＿＿＿＿＿＿＿＿＿＿＿＿＿＿

E. Translate the following into Chinese. (PRESENTATIONAL)

1. The weather forecast on the internet just said that it will not only be very cold tomorrow but it will also snow.

＿＿＿＿＿＿＿＿＿＿＿＿＿＿＿＿＿＿＿＿＿＿＿＿＿＿＿

＿＿＿＿＿＿＿＿＿＿＿＿＿＿＿＿＿＿＿＿＿＿＿＿＿＿＿

2. My older sister likes to shop. She bought a white shirt two weeks ago. Last week she bought a pair of blue pants. She liked them very much, so yesterday she bought another pair. She said she would like a pair of black shoes. This afternoon she'll go out shopping again. She really has a lot of money.

_____

_____

_____

_____

_____

F. Compare two of your favorite or least favorite celebrities in the same field or profession. Based on your previous knowledge and information you can find online, describe who's younger, taller, richer, who's more beautiful/handsome, and who is better at singing, dancing, playing sports, etc. (PRESENTATIONAL)

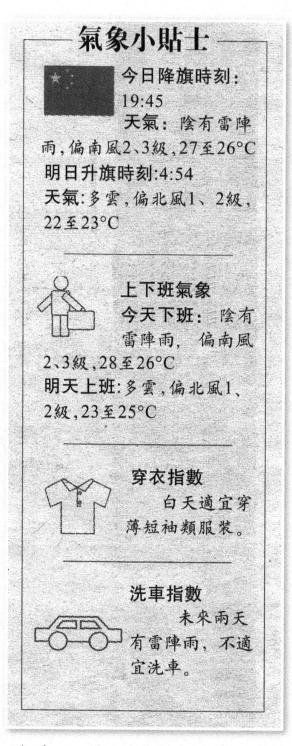

氣象小貼士

今日降旗時刻：19:45

天氣：陰有雷陣雨，偏南風2、3級，27至26℃

明日升旗時刻:4:54

天氣：多雲，偏北風1、2級，22至23℃

上下班氣象

今天下班：陰有雷陣雨，偏南風2、3級，28至26℃

明天上班:多雲，偏北風1、2級，23至25℃

穿衣指數

白天適宜穿薄短袖類服裝。

洗車指數

未來兩天有雷陣雨，不適宜洗車。

In addition to a weather forecast, what other advice does this newspaper clipping give?

Dialogue II: The Weather Here Is Awful

PART TWO

I. Listening Comprehension

A. Textbook Dialogue (True/False) (INTERPRETIVE)

( ) **1.** Gao Wenzhong and Bai Ying'ai are talking on the phone.
( ) **2.** Bai Ying'ai is surfing the internet for weather information.
( ) **3.** Gao Wenzhong is moving to California for its good weather.
( ) **4.** Bai Ying'ai is interviewing for a job in New York because she does not like California.
( ) **5.** Bai Ying'ai will cut her trip short because she can't stand the local weather anymore.

B. Workbook Dialogue (Multiple Choice) (INTERPRETIVE)

( ) **1.** It's been raining since at least yesterday.
( ) **2.** The woman likes rainy weather.
( ) **3.** The woman is from another city.
( ) **4.** The man doesn't care whether the woman stays or not.
( ) **5.** The woman probably would consider watching a different DVD with the man.

C. Listening Rejoinder (INTERPERSONAL)

In this section, you will hear two speakers talking. After hearing the first speaker, select the best from the four possible responses given by the second speaker.

II. Speaking Exercises

A. Answer the questions in Chinese based on the Textbook Dialogue. (INTERPRETIVE/PRESENTATIONAL)

1. How did Gao Wenzhong and Bai Ying'ai communicate with each other?
2. Why didn't Bai Ying'ai go out?
3. What kept Bai Ying'ai from going home?
4. Does Bai Ying'ai think that the weather in California is nice? Does she want to go there? Why or why not?

B. Ask your partner what his/her favorite city is and to describe what the weather is like there (in each season). (INTERPERSONAL)

III. Reading Comprehension (INTERPRETIVE)

A. Building Words

If you combine the *yǔ* in *xià yǔ* with the *yī* in *yīfu*, you have *yǔyī*, as seen in #1 below. Can you guess what the word *yǔyī* means? Complete this section by providing the characters, the *pinyin* and the English equivalent of each new word formed this way. You may consult a dictionary if necessary.

	new word	*pinyin*	English
1. "下雨"的"雨"+"衣服"的"衣" → 雨+衣 →	_____	_____	_____
2. "下雨"的"雨"+"鞋" → 雨+鞋 →	_____	_____	_____
3. "一枝筆"的"筆"+"考試"的"試" → 筆+試 →	_____	_____	_____
4. "回去"的"回"+"一封信"的"信" → 回+信 →	_____	_____	_____
5. "寒假"的"寒"+"冬天"的"冬" → 寒+冬 →	_____	_____	_____

B. Read the passage and answer the questions (True/False).

　　黃先生以前在加州工作。加州冬天不冷，夏天不熱，春天和秋天更舒服。黃先生現在在紐約工作。他說紐約夏天很熱，春天秋天也不太舒服，冬天天氣更糟糕，不但很冷，而且常常下雪。他約夏小姐這個週末去加州玩兒，夏小姐說加州天氣好是好，可是沒意思。

( ) **1.** Mr. Huang used to work in California.

( ) **2.** The four seasons were equally comfortable in New York.

( ) **3.** In New York, winter is the worst season.

( ) **4.** Mr. Huang would like to spend a weekend in California.

( ) **5.** Ms. Xia declined Mr. Huang's invitation because she liked the weather in her own city better.

C. Read the passage and answer the questions (True/False).

　　謝小姐是北京人，在加州工作。她的爸爸媽媽都在北京，謝小姐常常去看他們。可是她不喜歡夏天回去，因為北京的夏天很熱。謝小姐想請她爸爸媽媽夏天到加州來，可是她的爸爸媽媽說，加州好是好，可是那兒的朋友比北京少得多。所以他們覺得北京雖然天氣不好，可是比加州更有意思。

( ) **1.** 謝小姐的爸爸媽媽常常去加州。

( ) **2.** 謝小姐常常在六月或者七月回北京。

( ) **3.** 謝小姐的爸爸媽媽在北京有很多朋友。

( ) **4.** 謝小姐覺得加州夏天的天氣比北京好。

( ) **5.** 謝小姐的爸爸媽媽很喜歡北京。

D. Read the following dialogue and answer the questions.

（老王和老李打電話聊天。）

老王：老李，我最近工作不忙，想去北京玩兒。

老李：現在是冬天，這兒天氣非常冷。

老王：春天呢？

老李：北京春天的天氣有的時候也很糟糕！

老王：夏天呢？

老李：夏天比春天更糟糕，不但很熱而且常常下雨。

老王：啊，冬天不好，春天不好，夏天也不好，你不希望
　　　我去北京，對嗎？

老李：不、不，你是我最好的朋友。我希望你秋天來，因
　　　為北京秋天最舒服。

老王：那好，我秋天去。

Questions: (True/False)

( ) **1.** The telephone conversation took place in the summer.
( ) **2.** Lao Li lives in Beijing.
( ) **3.** According to Lao Li, the best season in Beijing is autumn.
( ) **4.** It is not very cold in winter in Beijing.
( ) **5.** Lao Li doesn't want Lao Wang to come to Beijing.

E. This sign indicates that this is a place for _____.

F. Answer the following questions based on the visual given.

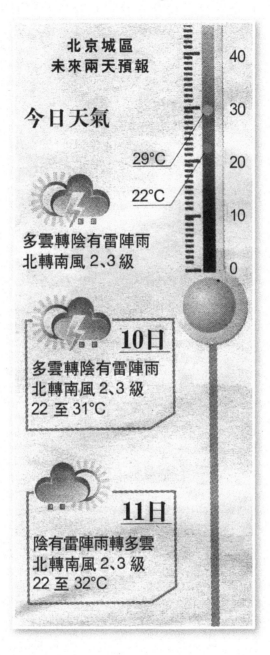

1. 這是哪一個城市的天氣預報？ _____

2. 哪一天最熱？ _____

3. 這幾天會不會下雨？ _____

IV. Writing Exercises

A. Building Characters

Form a character by fitting the given components together as indicated. Then provide a word or phrase in which that character appears.

EXAMPLE: a 日 on the left with a 月 on the right: It is the character <u>明</u> as in <u>明天</u>.

1. a 力 on the left with a 口 on the right: It is the character _____ as in _____.

2. a three-dot water radical on the left with the 先 in 先生: It is the character _____

   as in _____.

3. a 女 on the left with a 口 on the right: It is the character _____ as in _____.

4. a 今 on the top with a 心 at the bottom: It is the character _____ as

   in _____.

5. a three-dot water radical on the left with the 票 in 機票 on the right: It is the

   character _____ as in _____.

B. Shoe shopping

Person A really likes this pair of shoes. She loves the color, the style, the fit, and the comfort, and would like to purchase them. But her mother, Person B, is only concerned about the price. What would you say to A in a diplomatic but honest way if you were B?

EXAMPLE: **A:** 這雙鞋的顏色真漂亮。

B: 顏色<u>漂亮是漂亮</u>，<u>可是太貴了</u>。

1. **A:** 這雙鞋的樣子真好看。

   B: 樣子_____，_____。

2. **A:** 這雙鞋的大小真合適。

   B: 大小_____，_____。

3. **A:** 這雙鞋真舒服。

   B: _____ , _____ 。

C. Little Zhang is a true fan of *Harry Potter*. He read it again and again during the winter break. Here's part of the reading log he kept.

December 26	December 27	December 28	December 29	December 30
Harry Potter	*Harry Potter*	*Harry Potter*	*Harry Potter*	*Harry Potter*
✓	✓	✗	✓	✓

小張十二月二十六日看了 *Harry Potter*，十二月二十七日又看

了 *Harry Potter*。

十二月二十八日 _____

十二月二十九日 _____

十二月三十日 _____

How about you? Are you a fan of *Harry Potter* or any other books, or are you enthusiastic about a particular movie, TV show, sports team, or musician? Write a recollection like the one above describing your repeated reading, viewing, or listening.

_____

_____

_____

_____

D. Translate the following into Chinese. (PRESENTATIONAL)

1. Shoot, today is even colder than yesterday! I'd better put on my new sweater, have some hot coffee, and tell my little brother not to go outside to play.

_____

_____

_____

2. I have three pairs of pants: one white, one black, and one brown. The white pants were $124.99 and are much more expensive than the black ones. The black ones are newer than the brown ones, but they are a little big on me. I think the brown ones fit me the best. They are not only good-looking but also inexpensive. I wore them three times last week. This week I wore them three times again. I want to wear them three more times next week.

_____

_____

_____

_____

_____

3. I like this school very much. It is big and beautiful. Everyone says it is as beautiful as a park. Many students ice skate in the winter. The weather forecast said it would be very cold and it would snow next week. I hope I can go skating next weekend.

_____

_____

_____

E. Write a weather forecast for tomorrow based on the clues given below. Focus your report on the possible changes in temperature and precipitation in the morning, afternoon, and late at night. (PRESENTATIONAL)

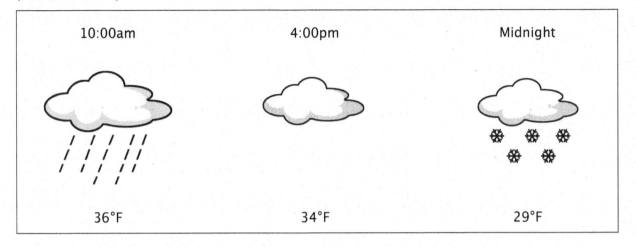

10:00am	4:00pm	Midnight
36°F	34°F	29°F

F. Check your local weather forecast for tomorrow, and report in writing whether it's predicted to rain, snow, and be warmer or colder than today. (PRESENTATIONAL)

G. Pick any two countries. Search online or in an encyclopedia to find out which country is bigger, which has a larger population (xxx 的人比 xxx 的人多), which country's summer is hotter, which country's winter is colder, which country's spring or fall is more pleasant, etc. Write a paragraph comparing the two countries. (PRESENTATIONAL)

H. Storytelling (PRESENTATIONAL)

Write a story in Chinese based on the four cartoons below. Make sure that your story has a beginning, middle, and end. Also make sure that the transition from one picture to the next is smooth and logical.

城市	天氣	最高氣溫	最低氣溫	城市	天氣	最高氣溫	最低氣溫
北京		31	22	石家莊		31	22
哈爾濱		27	18	濟南		30	22
長春		27	19	鄭州		28	20
沈陽		28	20	合肥		29	24
天津		31	22	南京		29	24
呼和浩特		27	16	上海		35	27
烏魯木齊		37	23	武漢		30	24
西寧		24	12	長沙		33	24
銀川		29	19	南昌		30	25
蘭州		31	19	杭州		35	25
西安		35	23	福州		36	27
拉薩		20	9	南寧		33	25
成都		32	24	海口		34	26
重慶		35	25	廣州		33	26

中國城市的天氣預報

LESSON 12 **Dining**
第十二課 吃飯

12

PART ONE **Dialogue I: Dining Out**

🔘 I. Listening Comprehension

A. Textbook Dialogue (Multiple Choice) (INTERPRETIVE)

Indicate the correct answer in the parentheses.

( ) **1.** **a.** Wang Peng and Li You did not have to wait to be seated.

   b. Wang Peng and Li You had to wait a long time for a table.

   c. The restaurant was not crowded at all.

   d. There was still a table available.

( ) **2.** **a.** Wang Peng and Li You ordered food separately.

   b. Li You asked Wang Peng to order for her.

   c. Wang Peng offered to order for Li You.

   d. Wang Peng did not want to order for Li You.

( ) **3.** **a.** The diners ordered two dishes plus soup.

   b. Wang Peng ordered three dishes and a soup.

   c. Li You did not order any soup.

   d. Wang Peng ordered two different soups for himself and Li You.

( ) **4.** **a.** Wang Peng did not want any ice in his beverage.

   b. Wang Peng asked for lots of ice in his beverage.

   c. Li You asked for lots of ice in her beverage.

   d. Wang Peng and Li You both wanted lots of ice in their beverages.

( ) **5. a.** Both Wang Peng and Li You are vegetarians.

     b. Li You is a vegetarian.

     c. Wang Peng prefers vegetarian dumplings.

     d. Li You occasionally eats meat.

B. Workbook Dialogue (True/False) (INTERPRETIVE)

( ) **1.** The man and the woman are at home.

( ) **2.** The woman has completely changed her diet.

( ) **3.** The woman suggests meat dumplings because she does not want to be difficult.

( ) **4.** The woman still doesn't eat meat at home.

( ) **5.** The man suggests vegetable dumplings because the woman is a vegetarian.

C. Listening Rejoinder (INTERPERSONAL)

In this section, you will hear two speakers talking. After hearing the first speaker, select the best from the four possible responses given by the second speaker.

II. Speaking Exercises

A. Answer the questions in Chinese based on the Textbook Dialogue. (INTERPRETIVE/PRESENTATIONAL)

1. What was Li You's impression when she entered the restaurant?
2. Was there meat in the dumplings or the tofu dish that Li You and Wang Peng ordered? Why or why not?
3. What special requests did Li You make for her hot and sour soup?
4. Did Li You and Wang Peng have any vegetable dishes? Why or why not?
5. What drinks did Li You and Wang Peng order?

B. Ask your partner what kinds of drinks he/she usually orders in a restaurant. (INTERPERSONAL)

C. With a partner, participate in a simulated conversation in a restaurant. One of you will be a customer and the other the waiter/waitress. The customer will order a main dish, a soup, and a drink and give special requests about the dish or the drink. The waiter/waitress recommends a dish, politely takes the order, and repeats what the customer wants at the end. (INTERPERSONAL)

III. Reading Comprehension (INTERPRETIVE)

A. Building Words

If you combine the *shū* in *kàn shū* with the *zhuō* in *zhuōzi*, you have *shūzhuō*, as seen in #1 below. Can you guess what the word *shūzhuō* means? Complete this section by providing the characters, the *pinyin* and the English equivalent of each new word formed this way. You may consult a dictionary if necessary.

	new word	*pinyin*	English

1. "看書" 的 "書" + "桌子" 的 "桌"

   → 書+桌 → _____ _____ _____

2. "吃飯" 的 "飯" + "桌子" 的 "桌"

   → 飯+桌 → _____ _____ _____

3. "青菜" 的 "菜" + "刀"

   → 菜+刀 → _____ _____ _____

4. "吃素" 的 "素" + "點菜" 的 "菜"

   → 素+菜 → _____ _____ _____

5. "喝茶" 的 "茶" + "飯館" 的 "館"

   → 茶+館 → _____ _____ _____

B. Read the dialogue below and answer the questions.

李小姐：服務員，你們的家常豆腐一點兒也不好吃。酸辣湯也很糟糕。我點菜的時候告訴你我不喜歡味精，可是好像還是放了很多味精。

服務員：對不起，小姐，可是菜你都吃完了。大家都說我們飯館兒的菜很不錯，有的菜六點鐘就賣完了。

李小姐：你自己覺得這兒的菜怎麼樣？

服務員：我不知道。

李小姐：你怎麼不知道？你在這兒工作，不在這兒吃飯

　　　　嗎？

服務員：我真的不知道，因為我和別的服務員都去別的飯

　　　　館兒吃飯。

Questions (Multiple Choice)

( ) **1.** Miss Li did not like the soup because _____.

    a. it was too hot

    b. it was too sour

    c. it was not cooked in the way she wanted

( ) **2.** What does the waiter suggest in his comment on the food?

    a. Since Miss Li finished the food, it must have been okay.

    b. Miss Li finished it even though it was not good.

    c. Because it was good, it had sold out.

( ) **3.** The waiter tried to defend his restaurant by saying that _____.

    a. some of its dishes often sold out very quickly

    b. some customers had to come early

    c. some dishes had to be cooked early

( ) **4.** Miss Li assumed that _____.

    a. the waiter did not have his meals in the restaurant, even though he worked there

    b. the waiter had his daily lunch in the restaurant since he worked there

    c. the waiter had his lunch in the restaurant when he did not work there

( ) **5.** How did the waiter like the food in his restaurant?

    a. He didn't like it, even though he ate it every day.

    b. He liked it, but was not allowed to eat there.

    c. He didn't know since he had never eaten at the restaurant.

C. Read the passage and answer the questions.

　　王朋和李友昨天晚上六點鐘到一家飯館兒吃飯。他們要了兩杯可樂。王朋點了一盤肉和一盤餃子。李友一點兒肉也不吃，所以只要了一盤豆腐。兩杯可樂很快就來了，可是到了七點半一盤菜都沒上。王朋問服務員："我們的菜做好了嗎？"服務員說："你們現在餓了嗎？"王朋和李友都說："我們都餓了。"服務員告訴他們："我們飯館兒跟別的飯館兒不一樣。要是你不太餓，你會覺得我們的菜一點兒也不好吃。要是你真餓了，才會覺得我們的菜特別好吃。所以我得等你們很餓了才上菜。"

Questions (True/False)

( ) **1.** Li You ordered a Coke and a vegetarian dish.

( ) **2.** Wang Peng and Li You waited for their drinks for a long time.

( ) **3.** At 7:30, there was still one dish that had not yet arrived.

( ) **4.** We can assume that Wang Peng and Li You will visit this restaurant again soon.

Questions (Multiple Choice)

( ) **5.** According to the waiter, this restaurant is different from others because ____.

    a. its tasty food makes customers feel even hungrier

    b. its customers can never have enough of its delicious food

    c. its food is tasty only to hungry customers

( ) **6.** According to the waiter, he had to ____.

    a. wait for Wang Peng and Li You to become really hungry

    b. wait on other hungry customers first

    c. eat first because he was hungry

D.

No0032733 價 目 表			
品　　　　名	單價	數　　　　量	金額
招 牌 鍋 貼	4		
韭 菜 鍋 貼	4		
辣 味 鍋 貼	5		
招 牌 水 餃	5		
韭 菜 水 餃	5		
辣 味 水 餃	5		
素　 水 餃	5		
鮮 蝦 水 餃	7		
湯 類			
酸　 辣　 湯	25		
玉 米 濃 湯	25		
旗 魚 丸 湯	25		
原 汁 豆 漿	15		
純 黑 豆 漿	15		
米　　　漿	15		
小　　　菜			

合 計 :＿＿＿＿＿＿＿＿

1. What can you order from this menu if you are a vegetarian?

2. How much is their hot and sour soup?

IV. Writing Exercises

A. Give the appropriate number, measure word, and noun for each picture. Each measure word can only be used once.

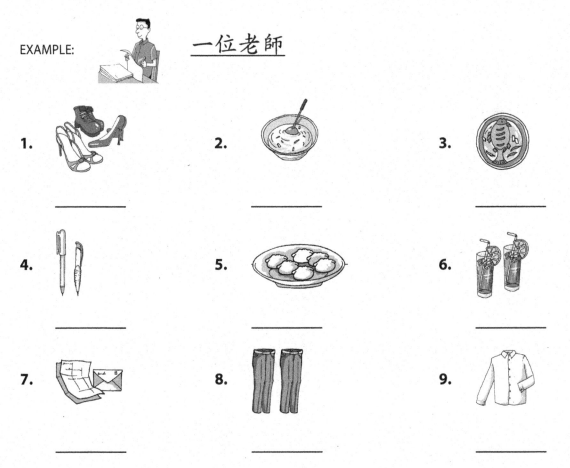

EXAMPLE: 一位老師

1. _____

2. _____

3. _____

4. _____

5. _____

6. _____

7. _____

8. _____

9. _____

B. This past winter break, Little Gao was too busy to do anything and had too little money to buy anything.

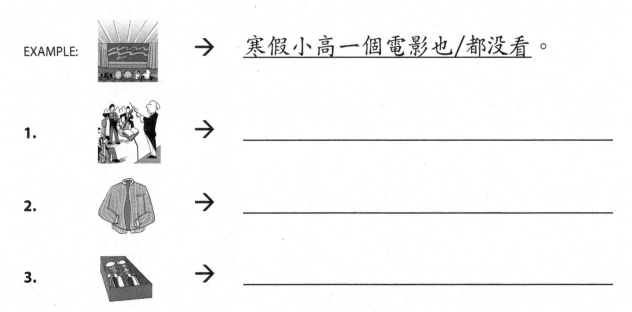

EXAMPLE: →   寒假小高一個電影也/都沒看。

1.   →   _____

2.   →   _____

3.   →   _____

C. Mr. Li is not feeling well and doesn't have an appetite for anything.

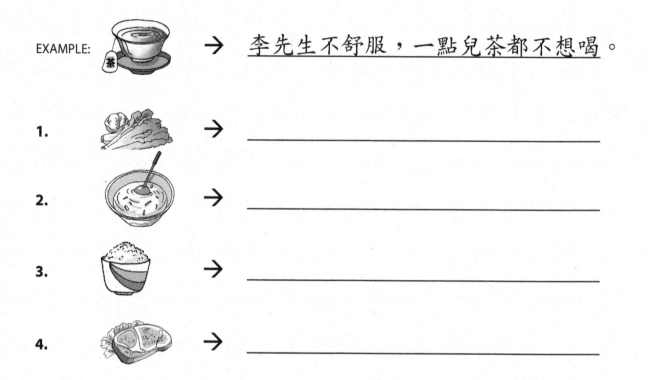

EXAMPLE: → 李先生不舒服，一點兒茶都不想喝。

1. → _____

2. → _____

3. → _____

4. → _____

D. Imagine that you're evaluating your own academic progress. If you wish to do better in school, what advice would you give yourself? What should you do more? What should you do less?

多⋯   少⋯

_____   _____

_____   _____

_____   _____

_____   _____

⋯   ⋯

E. In Other Words

Little Wang always listens to his mother. If his mother says: "要是功課沒做好，就不能玩兒，" he knows it means, in other words, "功課做好了，才能玩兒。" Let's see what other parental directions Little Wang listens to.

1. 要是飯沒吃完，就不能玩兒。

In other words: _____

2. 要是漢字沒寫對，就不能玩兒。

In other words: _____

3. 要是錄音沒聽懂，就不能玩兒。

In other words: _____

4. 要是考試沒準備好，就不能玩兒。

In other words: _____

F. Translate the following into Chinese. (PRESENTATIONAL)

1.　A: Do you use MSG when you cook?

_____

　B: No, I don't. Not even a bit.

_____

2.　A: Eat some more. Aren't you hungry?

_____

　B: I am hungry. But I am a vegetarian.

_____

　A: Is that right? I'll make some vegetable dumplings. They will be ready in no time.

_____

　B: Thank you.

_____

這些是豆腐。

PART TWO Dialogue II: Eating in a Cafeteria

I. Listening Comprehension

A. Textbook Dialogue (True/False) (INTERPRETIVE)

( ) **1.** There was nothing good to eat in the student cafeteria.

( ) **2.** The sweet and sour fish was very tasty.

( ) **3.** Wang Peng didn't like the chef's recommendation.

( ) **4.** Wang Peng didn't have any cash on him.

( ) **5.** The chef shortchanged Wang Peng.

B. Workbook Dialogue (Multiple Choice) (INTERPRETIVE)

( ) **1.** Who will cook tonight?

  a. The woman will do all the cooking tonight.
  b. The woman will do most of the cooking tonight.
  c. The man will do all the cooking tonight.
  d. The man will do most of the cooking tonight.

( ) **2.** Who wants soup?

  a. the man
  b. the woman
  c. both the man and the woman
  d. neither the man nor the woman

( ) **3.** Which of the following statements is true?

  a. The man will make the soup.
  b. The woman will make the soup.
  c. The man and the woman will make the soup together.
  d. The man and the woman will each make their own soup.

( ) **4.** The woman offers to make the soup because _____.

  a. the man doesn't know how to make it
  b. she doesn't like how the man makes it
  c. she wants to help
  d. the man doesn't feel like making soup

C. Listening Rejoinder (INTERPERSONAL)

In this section, you will hear two speakers talking. After hearing the first speaker, select the best from the four possible responses given by the second speaker.

_____

II. Speaking Exercises

A. Answer the questions in Chinese based on the Textbook Dialogue. (INTERPRETIVE/PRESENTATIONAL)

1. How did the chef describe the fish in sweet and sour sauce?
2. Did Wang Peng order the beef braised in soy sauce?
3. What did Wang Peng finally order?
4. What was the amount of change that the chef gave to Wang Peng and why?

B. Ask your friend how much he/she usually spends on lunch. (INTERPERSONAL)

C. With a partner, participate in a simulated conversation. You ask your partner (a waiter in a restaurant) the total cost of your order. He/she tells you the price and you pay with an approximate amount of cash. He/she gives you the wrong amount of change, either more or less than what should be given. Politely explain to him/her how the amount of change is wrong. (INTERPERSONAL)

III. Reading Comprehension

A. Building Words

If you combine the *mǐ* in *mǐfàn* with the *cù* in *tángcùyú*, you have *mǐcù*, as seen in #1 below. Can you guess what the word *mǐcù* means? Complete this section by providing the characters, the *pinyin* and the English equivalent of each new word formed this way. You may consult a dictionary if necessary.

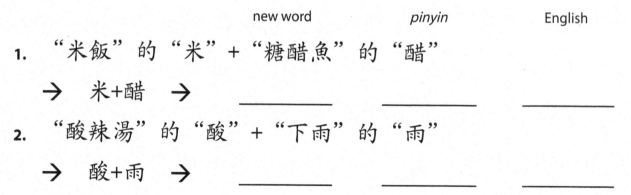

	new word	*pinyin*	English
1. "米飯"的"米" + "糖醋魚"的"醋" → 米+醋 →	_____	_____	_____
2. "酸辣湯"的"酸" + "下雨"的"雨" → 酸+雨 →	_____	_____	_____

3. "金" + "糖醋魚" 的 "魚"

   → 金+魚 → _____ _____ _____

4. "涼拌" 的 "涼" + "鞋"

   → 涼+鞋 → _____ _____ _____

5. "喝水" 的 "水" + "牛肉" 的 "牛"

   → 水+牛 → _____ _____ _____

B. Read the dialogue and answer the questions. (INTERPRETIVE)

李先生：請問，你們的紅燒牛肉怎麼樣？

服務員：好吃極了。

李先生：你們的家常豆腐好不好？

服務員：家常豆腐比紅燒牛肉更好吃。

李先生：那你們的糖醋魚呢？

服務員：糖醋魚比家常豆腐更好吃。

李先生：你們的菜都好吃，那我點什麼呢？還是給我一盤
　　　　紅燒牛肉吧。

服務員：好，紅燒牛肉比糖醋魚更好吃。

李先生：你剛才說家常豆腐比紅燒牛肉更好吃。算了吧，
　　　　我不點菜了。我去別的飯館吧。

服務員：先生，為什麼？

李先生：因為你不知道哪個菜好吃。

Questions (True/False)

( ) **1.** Mr. Li was very familiar with the menu.

( ) **2.** The waiter believed that beef in soy sauce was the most delicious dish on the menu.

( ) **3.** Mr. Li was most likely a vegetarian.

( ) **4.** In the end, Mr. Li did not eat at this restaurant.

Questions (Multiple Choice)

( ) **5.** Which of the following statements is true?

    a. The waiter was genuinely enthusiastic about the food in his restaurant.

    b. The waiter tried to familiarize Mr. Li with the menu.

    c. The waiter tried to push Mr. Li for a quick order.

( ) **6.** Mr. Li decided to eat elsewhere because

    a. he was overwhelmed by all the choices at the restaurant.

    b. he lost count of the number of dishes.

    c. he realized that the service there was too slow.

C. Answer the questions based on the reading passage.

小謝和小張剛打完球，現在又餓又渴。他們走進一家餐廳，想點些吃的和喝的東西。可是他們兩個人一共只有三十二塊五毛錢。他們最少得點一個素菜，一個葷菜（hūncài, 有肉的菜），一碗湯，兩碗飯，兩個人還得喝點東西。不過小謝不吃辣的菜，小張不能喝茶或者咖啡。要是你是小謝或者小張，你怎麼辦？下邊是餐廳的菜單，請你看一下，然後告訴師傅你們想吃什麼，喝什麼。

菜單

素餃子	6.25	（一盤）
牛肉餃子	6.75	（一盤）
紅燒牛肉	7.95	
糖醋牛肉	7.75	
紅燒魚	8.75	
糖醋魚	8.75	
*家常豆腐	6.50	
紅燒豆腐	6.50	
*涼拌黃瓜	6.25	
白菜豆腐湯	3.75	（兩人份）
白飯	0.75	
可樂	1.50	
綠茶	1.25	
紅茶	1.25	
咖啡	1.25	

＊＝辣的菜

看了菜單以後，現在請你幫小謝和小張點菜。

點菜單

第一道菜：	_____	$_____
第二道菜：	_____	$_____
第三道菜：	_____	$_____
湯：	_____	$_____
喝的東西：	_____	$_____
飯：	_____	$_____
		$_____

D. Read the passage below. Then answer the first two questions in English, and the third in Chinese. (INTERPRETIVE/PRESENTATIONAL)

小夏渴極了，也餓極了。他走進飯館，想點一杯涼涼的、甜甜的可樂。可是，上個星期醫生告訴他得少喝甜的東西。他又想點茶或者咖啡，也不行，因為喝了會讓他緊張。那來碗酸辣湯吧！可是醫生說他一點兒辣的都不能吃。算了，算了，多喝水吧！小夏想點牛肉，不過，最近牛肉好像有問題。那還是吃魚吧！可是服務員告訴他魚賣完了。糟糕！那吃什麼呢？ 最後，小夏點了一盤素餃子，一盤豆腐，一盤涼拌黃瓜。吃完以後，小夏覺得不夠，還覺得餓。要是你是小夏，這個時候你怎麼辦？

1. List on the left all the drinks and the dishes that Little Xia wished to order but didn't, and explain on the right why he didn't.

_____   _____

_____   _____

_____   _____

_____   _____

_____   _____

2. What did Little Xia end up having at the restaurant? Do you like his choices? Why or why not?

_____

3. Answer the question at the end of the story.

_____

E. Look at the prices displayed and answer the following question.

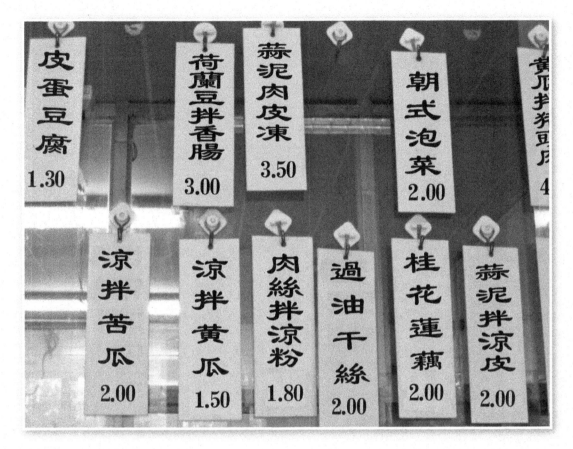

How much is the cucumber salad? _____

F. Read the notice posted and answer the following question.

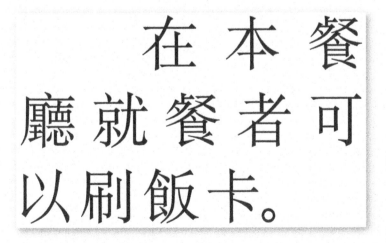

在本餐廳就餐者可以刷飯卡。

Can one use meal cards in this particular cafeteria? _____

IV. Writing Exercises

A. Building Characters

Form a character by fitting the given components together as indicated. Then provide a word, a phrase, or a short sentence in which that character appears.

EXAMPLE: a 口 on the left with a 加 as in 加州: It is the character <u>咖</u> as in <u>咖啡</u>.

1. a 口 on the top with a 貝 at the bottom: It is the character _____ as

   in _____.

2. a 米 as in 米飯 on the left with a 青 as in 青菜 on the right: It is the character

   _____ as in _____.

3. a side 食 radical on the left with a 我 on the right: It is the character _____ as

   in _____.

4. a three-dot water radical on the left with a 青 as in 青菜 on the right: It is the

   character _____ as in _____.

5. a three-dot water on the left with a 每 as in 每天 on the right: It is the character

   _____ as in _____.

B. Everyone's palate and dietary restrictions are different. According to your own preferences, what will you say to the waiter when you order dishes? 多放 (duō fàng)…or 少放 (shǎo fàng)…

(PRESENTATIONAL)

_____   _____

_____   _____

_____   _____

...   ...

C. Place your order based on the illustrations given. (PRESENTATIONAL)

EXAMPLE: → 服務員，來兩碗米飯。

1. → _____ 。

2. → _____ 。

3. → _____ 。

4. → _____ 。

D. What First Comes to Mind: When hearing 酸辣湯, many people who like that soup will immediately think of the expression 酸酸的、辣辣的，很好喝. How about the following? (INTERPRETIVE/PRESENTATIONAL)

1. 糖醋魚： _____

2. 涼拌豆腐： _____

3. 冰咖啡： _____

E. Answer the following questions based on your own situation. (INTERPERSONAL)

1. A: 你覺得中國菜好吃還是美國菜好吃？

B: _____

2. **A:** 你喜歡吃青菜還是吃肉？

   B: _____

3. **A:** 天氣熱的時候，你喜歡喝什麼？

   B: _____

4. **A:** 你平常先喝湯再吃飯，還是先吃飯再喝湯？

   B: _____

5. **A:** 你能吃辣的嗎？

   B: _____

6. **A:** 要是你不能吃味精，你跟服務員說什麼？

   B: _____

F. Translate the following into Chinese. (PRESENTATIONAL)

1. **A:** We just finished our exam. I asked Xiao Li to have dinner with us tomorrow.

   _____

   B: Great! What should we make then?

   _____

   A: He likes to eat meat. We'll make beef in soy sauce, and sweet and sour fish. How's that?

   _____

   B: You are a vegetarian. I'll make some vegetarian dumplings and a cucumber salad.

   _____

   A: Good. Xiao Li likes vegetarian dumplings and cucumber salad, too.

   _____

2. Yesterday was Little Wang's birthday. I treated him to dinner. We went to a Chinese restaurant. When we got there, there wasn't even a single customer. The waiter asked us what we would like to eat. I ordered a plate of dumplings. Little Wang said he was hungry and thirsty. He ordered a Coke, a tofu dish, and a sweet and sour fish. The waiter wanted us to order one more dish. We said we'd already ordered enough food. But the dumplings were all sold out and the fish was too sour. The waiter not only served the food slowly, but also gave the wrong change. The service there was really terrible. We'd better not go there any more in the future.

G. Today's Special (PRESENTATIONAL)

Pretend that you're a restaurant manager. Make a flier to promote your specials of the day. The flier has to include one spicy dish, one meat dish, one vegetable dish, and one soup. Make sure to include wording that promotes your dishes on the flier, and don't forget to mention that you don't put any MSG in your dishes.

H. Storytelling (PRESENTATIONAL)

Write a story based on the four cartoons below. Make sure that your story has a beginning, middle and end. Also make sure that the transition from one picture to the next is smooth and logical.

13 LESSON 13 **Asking Directions**
第十三課 問路

| **PART ONE** | **Dialogue I: Where Are You Off To?** |

🔘 I. Listening Comprehension

A. Textbook Dialogue (Multiple Choice) (INTERPRETIVE)

( ) **1.** Chang Laoshi asks Bai Ying'ai where she is going because

  a. Chang Laoshi is nosy.
  b. this is a common greeting.
  c. Chang Laoshi needs to know where Little Bai is going.
  d. Bai Ying'ai looks lost.

( ) **2.** Does Bai Ying'ai know how to get to the computer center?

  a. No, Bai Ying'ai doesn't know how to get to the computer center.
  b. No, Bai Ying'ai has forgotten how to get to the computer center.
  c. No, Bai Ying'ai has no idea where the computer center is.
  d. No, and Chang Laoshi doesn't know how to get to the computer center, either.

( ) **3.** Which description of the campus is correct?

  a. The library is between the computer center and the student activity center.
  b. The student activity center is between the library and the computer center.
  c. The computer center is between the library and the student activity center.
  d. The computer center is between Wang Peng's dorm and the library.

( ) **4.** Chang Laoshi and Bai Ying'ai will walk together because

  a. Chang Laoshi enjoys Bai Ying'ai's company.
  b. Chang Laoshi's destination is not far away from Bai Ying'ai's.
  c. Bai Ying'ai asks Chang Laoshi to.
  d. they haven't seen each other for a long time.

B. Workbook Dialogue (True/False) (INTERPRETIVE)

( ) The woman doesn't know where the athletic field is.

( ) The man doesn't know where the computer center is.

( ) The woman is on her way to the computer center.

( ) The athletic field is between the library and the computer center.

C. Listening Rejoinder (INTERPERSONAL)

In this section, you will hear two speakers talking. After hearing the first speaker, select the best from the four possible responses given by the second speaker.

_____

II. Speaking Exercises

A. Answer the questions in Chinese based on the Textbook Dialogue. (INTERPRETIVE/PRESENTATIONAL)

1. Where did Bai Ying'ai want to go?
2. Which place is farther from the classroom, the computer center or the athletic field?
3. Where is the computer center?
4. Why did Teacher Chang suggest that Bai Ying'ai and she should go together?

B. Draw a simple map of your school's campus and indicate the locations of the library, student activity center, your Chinese classroom, the computer center, and the athletic field in relation to each other. With a partner, do a role play. Pretend you are a new student and ask your partner where the school library and the student activity center are. (INTERPERSONAL)

III. Reading Comprehension (INTERPRETIVE)

A. Building Words

If you combine the *jìn* in *yuǎnjìn* with the *lù* in *gāosù gōnglù*, you have *jìnlù*, as seen in #1 below. Can you guess what the word *jìnlù* means? Complete this section by providing the characters, the *pinyin*, and the English equivalent of each new word formed this way. You may consult a dictionary if necessary.

	new word	*pinyin*	English
1. "遠近"的"近" + "高速公路"的"路" → 近+路 →	_____	_____	_____
2. "運動"的"動" + "生詞"的"詞" → 動+詞 →	_____	_____	_____

3. "遠近" 的 "遠" + "電視" 的 "視"

    → 遠+視 → ＿＿＿＿＿ ＿＿＿＿＿ ＿＿＿＿＿

4. "遠近" 的 "近" + "電視" 的 "視"

    → 近+視 → ＿＿＿＿＿ ＿＿＿＿＿ ＿＿＿＿＿

5. "書店" 的 "店" + "服務員" 的 "員"

    → 店+員 → ＿＿＿＿＿ ＿＿＿＿＿ ＿＿＿＿＿

B. Read the following passage and answer the questions.

小錢的家離學校很遠。每天早上，他都得先坐公共汽車，然後坐地鐵，才能到學校。因為每天去學校上課都得花很多時間，所以他覺得很累，希望能換一個學校。他希望新學校離家近一點兒。

Questions: (True/False)

(　) **1.** Little Qian lives in a student dorm.
(　) **2.** Little Qian's home is on the subway line.
(　) **3.** The destination of his bus ride is the subway station.
(　) **4.** Little Qian doesn't mind the commute.
(　) **5.** If he could, Little Qian would like to go to a different school.

C. Read the following passage and answer the questions.

藍先生早上想到學校運動場去運動，可是他不知道運動場在哪兒。八點鐘，他在圖書館前邊看到李友，問李友運動場在哪兒，比書店近還是比書店遠？李友告訴他運動場沒有書店那麼遠。藍先生走到了書店，可是沒有看到運動場。書店的售貨員告訴他，運動場就在電腦中心的旁邊。藍先生到了電腦中心，也沒找到運動場，因為他不知道學校有兩個書店和兩個電腦中心。九點鐘藍先生又回到了圖書館。李友問："您去運動場運動了嗎？"藍先生說："不運動了，我今天已經走夠了。"

Questions (True/False)

( ) **1.** Mr. Lan does not know the campus well.
( ) **2.** Mr. Lan went to the library with Li You.
( ) **3.** According to Li You, Mr. Lan should see the athletic field before the bookstore.
( ) **4.** It is likely that Li You was in the library for at least an hour.
( ) **5.** In the end, Mr. Lan didn't want to go to the athletic field anymore because he had enough exercise already trying to find it.
( ) **6.** Mr. Lan didn't find the athletic field because of a miscommunication.

D. Look at the map and answer the question.

第一教學樓離圖書館近還是第二教學樓離圖書館近？

_____

IV. Writing Exercises

A. For each pair of pictures, write two sentences describing Little Gao's opinions.

EXAMPLE: delicious

→ <u>小高覺得餃子比米飯好吃。</u>
<u>小高覺得米飯沒有餃子好吃。</u>

1.   difficult

→ _____

_____

2.   fun/interesting

→ _____

_____

3.   expensive

→ _____

_____

B. List the activities that students can do at the student center at your school.

EXAMPLE: 學生可以到學生活動中心去運動。

1. _____

2. _____

3. _____

4. _____

5. _____

...

C. Imagine that you are a campus planner. Draw a plan of an ideal school. Where would you situate the library, classrooms, dorms, teachers' office building, computer center, and athletic facilities in relation to one another? Explain why in Chinese. (PRESENTATIONAL)

_____

_____

_____

D. Translate the following into Chinese. (PRESENTATIONAL)

1. **A:** Is the bookstore between the student center and the athletic field?

   _____

   B: No, it's inside that dorm.

   _____

2. **A:** I heard the park isn't far away from here. Do you know how to get there?

   _____

   B: Yes, I do. I'm heading there, too. Let's go together.

   _____

   A: Great!

   _____

PART TWO   Dialogue II: Going to Chinatown

I. Listening Comprehension

A. Textbook Dialogue (Multiple Choice) (INTERPRETIVE)

( ) **1.** Who has been to Chinatown before?

a. Both Wang Peng and Gao Wenzhong have been to Chinatown many times.
b. Wang Peng has been to Chinatown before.
c. Neither Gao Wenzhong nor Wang Peng has been to Chinatown before.
d. Gao Wenzhong has been to Chinatown before.

( ) **2.** Do they have a map?

a. Wang Peng has a map in his car.
b. Gao Wenzhong brought a map.
c. Gao Wenzhong forgot to bring a map.
d. Wang Peng doesn't need a map.

( ) **3.** Where do they end up?

a. in Chinatown
b. back at Wang Peng's place
c. at a traffic light
d. in Little Tokyo

B. Workbook Dialogue (Multiple Choice) (INTERPRETIVE)

( ) **1.** Where did the speakers think they were heading?

a. a restaurant in Beijing
b. a restaurant in Tokyo
c. a restaurant called Beijing
d. a restaurant called Tokyo

( ) **2.** The woman worried that they might not be able to get a seat in the restaurant because

a. it would take another six blocks to get to the restaurant.
b. it was Friday and a lot of people were dining out.
c. the restaurant didn't take reservations.
d. no one answered the phone at the restaurant.

( ) **3.** They end up having Japanese food because

    a. they had Chinese food last weekend.

    b. they are going to Tokyo soon.

    c. the man called the wrong restaurant.

    d. the Japanese restaurant is closer.

C. Listening Rejoinder (INTERPERSONAL)

In this section, you will hear two speakers talking. After hearing the first speaker, select the best from the four possible responses given by the second speaker.

———————————

II. Speaking Exercises

A. Answer the questions in Chinese based on the Textbook Dialogue. (INTERPRETIVE/PRESENTATIONAL)

1. Why didn't Wang Peng know where Chinatown was?

2. Did Wang Peng and Gao Wenzhong have a map with them? Why or why not?

3. What directions did Gao Wenzhong give Wang Peng to get to Chinatown?

4. Why didn't they make a turn at the fourth intersection?

5. Did Wang Peng and Gao Wenzhong arrive in Chinatown? Why or why not?

B. Ask your partner if he/she has ever been to a Chinatown. If so, ask what he/she did there. If not, ask how he/she would like to spend a day in Chinatown. (INTERPERSONAL)

C. Tell your classmates how to get to your place from school. Draw a map to illustrate the route. (PRESENTATIONAL)

III. Reading Comprehension (INTERPRETIVE)

A. Building Words

If you combine the *zuǒ* in *zuǒbian* with *shǒu*, you have *zuǒshǒu*, as seen in #1 below. Can you guess what the word *zuǒshǒu* means? Complete this section by providing the characters, the *pinyin*, and the English equivalent of each new word formed this way. You may consult a dictionary if necessary.

	new word	*pinyin*	English

1. "左邊" 的 "左" + "手"

   → 左+手 → _____ _____ _____

2. "右邊" 的 "右" + "手"

   → 右+手 → _____ _____ _____

3. "前面" 的 "前" + "門"

   → 前+門 → _____ _____ _____

4. "紅綠燈" 的 "紅" + "冰茶" 的 "茶"

   → 紅+茶 → _____ _____ _____

5. "紅綠燈" 的 "綠" + "冰茶" 的 "茶"

   → 綠+茶 → _____ _____ _____

B. Answer the following questions according to the map of the campus.

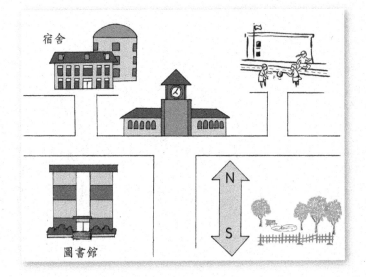

Questions: (True/False)

( ) 1. 學生宿舍的東邊有一個公園。

( ) 2. 圖書館在學生宿舍的南邊。

( ) 3. 學生宿舍在運動場的西邊。

( ) 4. 公園的北邊有公共汽車站。

C. Read the following passage and answer the questions.

　　老李去過中國城買東西、吃中國飯，但是每次都是坐朋友的車去。上個週末老李自己開車到中國城去,車裏沒有地圖,他走錯了。他想回家去拿地圖，可是找不到回家的路。他想問問朋友，可是沒有手機。老李很緊張，就到旁邊的飯館兒問。飯館兒的師傅告訴他一直往東開，過三個紅綠燈就能看到中國城了。

1. What had Old Li done in Chinatown in the past?
2. How did he go to Chinatown in the past?
3. Why couldn't he locate Chinatown last weekend?
4. Why didn't he go home for a map?
5. Why didn't he call someone for help?
6. Who gave him directions?
7. How did he finally find Chinatown?

D. Read the following passage and answer the questions.

　　快考試了，我得去書店買書復習復習，但我沒去過書店。小白說走到那裏太慢，開車很快就能到。她說從學校出來，先上大學路，一直往南開，到第一個紅綠燈往東開。然後到了第一個路口往左一拐就會看到路的右邊有一家活動中心。再往前走，過一個中國飯館就會看到路的左邊有一家鞋店，書店就在鞋店的旁邊。

1. What did the narrator want to buy? Why was she so anxious?

   _____

2. According to Little Bai, which way was more convenient to go to the narrator's destination, driving or walking?

   _____

3. Based on Little Bai's directions, draw a map of the route to the narrator's destination and indicate all the landmarks.

   _____

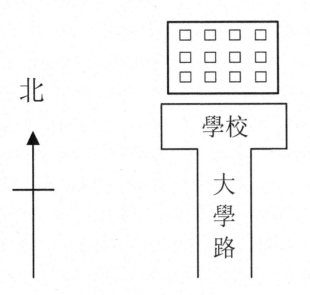

E. Look at the map and answer the question in Chinese.

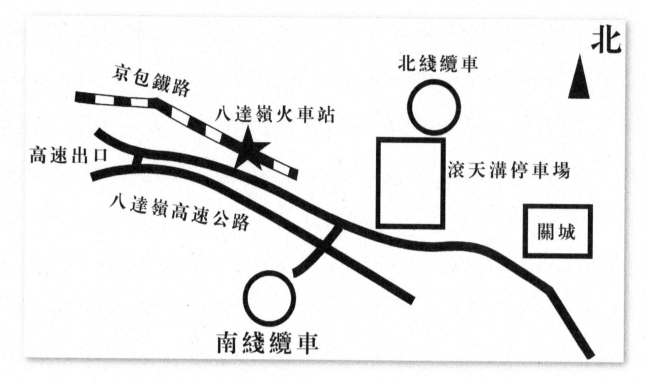

Is the train station to the north, east, south, or west of the highway?_____

IV. Writing Exercises

A. Building Characters

Form a character by fitting the given components together as indicated. Then provide a word or phrase in which that character appears.

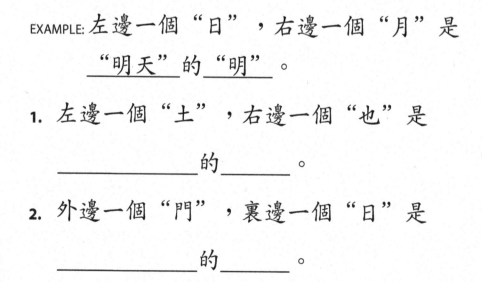

EXAMPLE: 左邊一個"日"，右邊一個"月"是

____明天____的____明____。

1. 左邊一個"土"，右邊一個"也"是

_____的_____。

2. 外邊一個"門"，裏邊一個"日"是

_____的_____。

3. 上邊一個"合適"的"合"，下邊一個"手"是

　　　　　　＿＿＿＿＿＿的＿＿＿。

4. 上邊一個"山"，下邊一個"山"是

　　　　　　＿＿＿＿＿＿的＿＿＿。

5. 上邊一個"口"，下邊一個"八"是

　　　　　　＿＿＿＿＿＿的＿＿＿。

B. Ask and answer the following questions based on your own experience.

EXAMPLE: cucumber salad

A: 你吃過涼拌黃瓜嗎？　　　　B: 我吃過。

A: 你覺得涼拌黃瓜好吃嗎？　　B: 我覺得涼拌黃瓜

　　　　　　　　　　　　　　　　很好吃/不好吃。

or

A: 你吃過涼拌黃瓜嗎？　　　　B: 我沒吃過。

A: 你想吃嗎？　　　　　　　　B: 我想吃/我不想吃。

1. family style tofu

　＿＿＿＿＿＿＿＿＿＿＿　　＿＿＿＿＿＿＿＿＿＿＿

2. sweet and sour fish

　＿＿＿＿＿＿＿＿＿＿＿　　＿＿＿＿＿＿＿＿＿＿＿

3. hot and sour soup

_____   _____

4. vegetable dumplings

_____   _____

5. baby bok choy

_____   _____

C. Using the table as a reference point, ask and answer where each item is located.

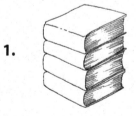

1.

_____

2.

_____

3.

_____

4.

_____

D. Locate the buildings based on the map.

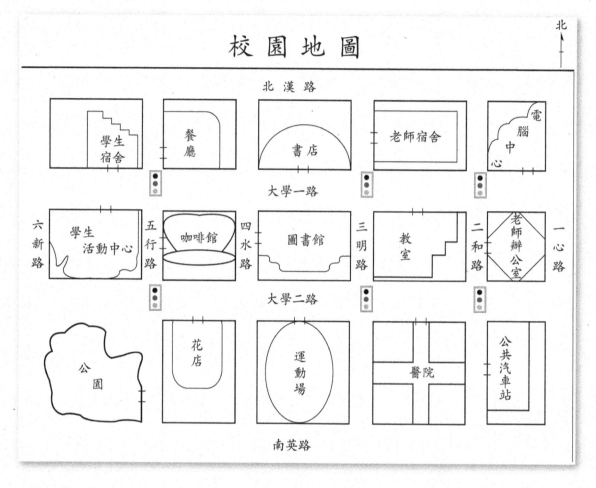

EXAMPLE: bookstore

A: 書店在哪兒？　　**B:** 書店在餐廳的東邊。／

　　　　　　　　　　　書店在老師宿舍的西邊。／

　　　　　　　　　　　書店在餐廳和老師宿舍的中間⋯

1. student activity center _____

2. teachers' offices _____

3. coffee shop _____

E. Answer the question based on the map.

請問，從公園到電腦中心怎麼走？

_____

_____

_____

F. Translate the following into Chinese. (PRESENTATIONAL)

1. A: Have you found your red shoes?

_____

B: No, I haven't.

_____

A: I heard your red shoes were expensive. A hundred dollars?

_____

B: Not that expensive.

_____

2. A: Have you finished the letter to your mother?

_____

B: No, I haven't finished. I haven't even started yet.

_____

A: Hurry up, her birthday is coming.

_____

B: Okay, I'll do it after I finish drinking this cup of coffee.

_____

3. A: Have you been to Chinatown?

_____

B: No, never. Where is it?

_____

A: It's not far from here. After two traffic lights, make a right turn, and you will be there. Would you like to go?

_____

B: Yes.

_____

A: Okay, let's go now.

_____

4. A: I am going to order the hot and sour soup today. What would you like to order?

_____

B: I've had their hot and sour soup before. It is a bit sour and a bit spicy. Quite delicious. But I've never had dumplings here. I am going to order some dumplings.

_____

_____

_____

G. Storytelling (PRESENTATIONAL)

Write a story based on the four cartoons below. Make sure that your story has a beginning, middle, and end. Also, make sure that the transition from one picture to the next is smooth and logical.

1

2

3

4

LESSON 14 **Birthday Party**
第十四課 生日晚會

| PART ONE | **Dialogue I: Let's Go to a Party!** |

I. Listening Comprehension

A. Textbook Dialogue (Multiple Choice) (INTERPRETIVE)

( ) **1.** Whose birthday is it?

   a. Gao Wenzhong's cousin's
   b. Gao Wenzhong's
   c. Gao Xiaoyin's
   d. Gao Xiaoyin's boyfriend's

( ) **2.** What will the host of the party *not* receive from Wang Peng and Li You?

   a. flowers
   b. fruit
   c. beverages
   d. balloons

( ) **3.** What will the host and guests *not* do at the party?

   a. sing
   b. dance
   c. watch a DVD
   d. eat

( ) **4.** Who will *not* be at the party?

   a. Gao Xiaoyin's boyfriend
   b. Gao Xiaoyin's classmate
   c. Gao Xiaoyin's cousin
   d. Gao Xiaoyin's parents

B. Workbook Narrative (INTERPRETIVE)

Answer the following question after listening to the short passage:

Who bought what? Match each of the persons with the right kind(s) of fruit:

C. Listening Rejoinder (INTERPERSONAL)

In this section, you will hear two speakers talking. After hearing the first speaker, select the best from the four possible responses given by the second speaker.

II. Speaking Exercises

A. Answer the questions in Chinese based on the Textbook Dialogue. (INTERPRETIVE/PRESENTATIONAL)

1. Why did Li You call Wang Peng?
2. What will people do at Gao Xiaoyin's place?
3. What will Wang Peng bring?
4. What will Li You bring and why?
5. How will Li You get to Gao Xiaoyin's place and why?

B. Do a role play with a partner. Invite your partner to your birthday party. Tell him/her when and where the party is, what people will do, what to bring, and how to get there. Ask your friend if he/she needs a ride. (INTERPERSONAL)

C. Tell your classmates about your favorite birthday party (including when and where the party was, what people did, and the reasons why it was your favorite). (PRESENTATIONAL)

III. Reading Comprehension (INTERPRETIVE)

A. Building Words

If you combine the *rè* in *tiānqi rè* with the *yǐn* in *yǐnliào*, you have *rèyǐn*, as seen in #1 below. Can you guess what the word *rèyǐn* means? Complete this section by providing the characters, the *pinyin*, and the English equivalent of each new word formed this way. You may consult a dictionary if necessary.

	new word	pinyin	English
1. "天氣熱" 的 "熱" + "飲料" 的 "飲" → 熱+飲 →	_____	_____	_____
2. "天氣冷" 的 "冷" + "飲料" 的 "飲" → 冷+飲 →	_____	_____	_____
3. "英國" 的 "國" + "一把花" 的 "花" → 國+花 →	_____	_____	_____
4. "門" + "路口" 的 "口" → 門+口 →	_____	_____	_____
5. "一把花" 的 "花" + "汽車" 的 "車" → 花+車 →	_____	_____	_____

B. Read the following passage and answer the questions.

　　昨天是小常二十歲生日，晚上我們在他的宿舍給他過生日。小常的女朋友帶了水果、飲料，還有很多好吃的東西。大家一邊吃東西、一邊聊天兒、一邊玩，晚上十二點才回家。因為我昨天回家太晚，所以今天的考試考得糟糕極了。

Questions (True/False)

( )**1.** Little Chang celebrated his nineteenth birthday last year.
( )**2.** Little Chang's girlfriend prepared snacks, fruit, and drinks for the party.
( )**3.** Everyone danced and had a great time last night.
( )**4.** The narrator didn't go to bed until after midnight.
( )**5.** The narrator did well on today's test.

C. Read the following dialogue and answer the questions.

（在李友的生日舞會上）

李友：小藍，喝點兒飲料或者吃點兒水果吧。

小藍：謝謝，我喝茶吧。李友，你看，張英正在跳舞呢。她穿的就是上個週末跟你一起買的那件襯衫，真漂亮。

李友：不對，她跟我一起買的那件是黃的。這件是白的，是你送給她的。你怎麼忘了？

小藍：是啊，我怎麼忘了呢？現在我知道我為什麼這麼喜歡這件襯衫了。

Questions (True/False)

( )**1.** Little Lan likes tea better than soda pop.
( )**2.** Li You went shopping with Zhang Ying last weekend.
( )**3.** Zhang Ying is wearing a yellow blouse for the party.
( )**4.** Zhang Ying bought a white blouse last weekend.
( )**5.** Little Lan forgot to give Zhang Ying a present.

D. This is the menu of a multi-course meal. Take a look and answer the following questions.

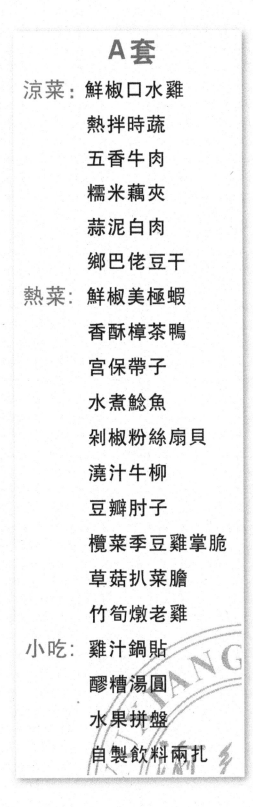

A套

涼菜： 鮮椒口水雞

熱拌時蔬

五香牛肉

糯米藕夾

蒜泥白肉

鄉巴佬豆干

熱菜： 鮮椒美極蝦

香酥樟茶鴨

宮保帶子

水煮鯰魚

剁椒粉絲扇貝

澆汁牛柳

豆瓣肘子

欖菜季豆雞掌脆

草菇扒菜膽

竹筍燉老雞

小吃： 雞汁鍋貼

醪糟湯圓

水果拼盤

自製飲料兩扎

1. Does the meal come with fruit and beverages? How do you know? _____

2. What do 涼菜 and 熱菜 refer to? _____

IV. Writing Exercises

A. Answer the following questions based on your own preferences.

1. 你愛吃什麼水果？

   _____

2. 你愛喝什麼飲料？

   _____

3. 你愛吃什麼中國菜？

   _____

B. Ask and answer questions based on the illustrations given.

EXAMPLE:

→A: 她（正在）做什麼呢？   B: 她（正在）跳舞呢。

1.    _____

   _____

2. _____

_____

3. _____

_____

C. You are planning a party and telling people what to bring.

EXAMPLE: → <u>王朋，請你帶蛋糕</u> (dàngāo)。

1. _____

2. _____

3. _____

D. Little Fei is an effusive guy. For example, he likes to say about the place he lives

➔ <u>我住的地方</u>好極了。(It's never just good, or even very good.)

What would he be likely to say about the following? Be sure to use a different adjective for each sentence:

1. the car he drives

_____

2. the computer he uses

_____

3. the characters he writes

_____

4. the friends he knows

_____

E. Translate the following into Chinese. (PRESENTATIONAL)

1. **A:** What kind of fruit do you like? Watermelon, pear, or apple?

_____

B: I love to eat watermelon in the summer, and apples in the fall.

_____

2. **A:** What are you doing?

_____

B: I'm watching TV.

_____

A: Gao Wenzhong is having a dance party. Do you feel like going?

_____

B: Sure, but his place is very far from my house. Can you come pick me up?

_____

A: No problem.

_____

B: Thanks. I'll wait for you downstairs in ten minutes.

_____

Dialogue II: Attending a Birthday Party

I. Listening Comprehension

A. Textbook Dialogue (Multiple Choice) (INTERPRETIVE)

( ) **1.** Who greeted Wang Peng and Li You at the door?

    a. Gao Wenzhong

    b. Gao Wenzhong's cousin

    c. Gao Xiaoyin

    d. Bai Ying'ai

( ) **2.** Who hadn't arrived yet?

    a. Wang Hong

    b. Helen

    c. Tom

    d. Bai Ying'ai

( ) **3.** Who is Tom?

    a. Helen's dog

    b. Helen's son

    c. Helen's boyfriend

    d. Helen's cousin

( ) **4.** Helen speaks Chinese very well because

    a. she is Chinese.

    b. she was a Chinese teacher.

    c. she studied Chinese in summer school.

    d. she has a lot of Chinese friends.

B. Workbook Dialogue (Multiple Choice) (INTERPRETIVE)

( ) **1.** The female speaker is the male speaker's _____.

    a. mother

    b. sister

    c. girlfriend

    d. cousin

( ) **2.** A book wouldn't be a good idea because

    a. the speaker's father doesn't have time to read.

    b. the speaker's father doesn't like to read.

    c. the speaker's father can't read.

    d. the speaker's father has too many books already.

( ) **3.** Coffee wouldn't make a good gift because

    a. the speaker's father doesn't like coffee.

    b. the speaker's father decided to give up caffeine.

    c. the speaker's father stopped drinking coffee on doctor's orders.

    d. the speaker's father is very picky about the coffee he drinks.

( ) **4.** A shirt wouldn't make a good present either because

    a. the speaker's father doesn't like others to buy clothes for him.

    b. the speaker's father doesn't wear dress shirts.

    c. the speaker's father doesn't need another shirt.

    d. it is impossible to find the right size for the father.

( ) **5.** What would the father like to have for his birthday?

    a. movies

    b. Chinese food

    c. time with his children

    d. time by himself

C. Workbook Narrative (INTERPRETIVE)

The speaker left a phone message for her dog sitter. You are going to hear part of the message. After listening to it, answer the following questions in English.

1. Does the speaker already know the dog sitter? How do you know?

_____

2. What specific instructions does the speaker give to the dog sitter? Please list them in detail.

_____

3. If you were the dog sitter, would you have any questions for the owner? Ask at least one.

_____

4. Has the dog sitter ever met the dog? How do you know?

_____

5. Would you dog-sit for the speaker if you were asked? Why or why not?

_____

D. Listening Rejoinder (INTERPERSONAL)

In this section, you will hear two speakers talking. After hearing the first speaker, select the best from the four possible responses given by the second speaker.

_____

II. Speaking Exercises

A. Answer the questions in Chinese based on the Textbook Dialogue. (INTERPRETIVE/PRESENTATIONAL)

1. What did Gao Xiaoyin say when she received the birthday presents from Li You and Wang Peng?
2. How much time does Wang Hong spend practicing English every day?
3. Who is Tom?
4. Where did Helen study Chinese?
5. What does Tom look like?

B. Work with a partner and ask each other how long you normally eat dinner, do homework, and sleep every day. (INTERPERSONAL)

C. Work with a partner and ask each other which year you were born in, where you were born, and your Chinese zodiac sign. (INTERPERSONAL)

D. Show a photo of someone famous, a family member, or a friend, and describe to your classmates what the person looks like. (PRESENTATIONAL)

III. Reading Comprehension (INTERPRETIVE)

A. Building Words

If you combine the *yǎn* in *yǎnjing* with the *qiú* in *dǎ qiú*, you have *yǎnqiú*, as seen in #1 below. Can you guess what the word *yǎnqiú* means? Complete this section by providing the characters, the *pinyin*, and the English equivalent of each new word formed this way. You may consult a dictionary if necessary.

	new word	*pinyin*	English

1. "眼睛" 的 "眼" + "打球" 的 "球"

   → 眼+球 → _____ _____ _____

2. "鼻子" 的 "鼻" + "發音" 的 "音"

   → 鼻+音 → _____ _____ _____

3. "蛋糕" 的 "蛋" + "白色" 的 "白"

   → 蛋+白 → _____ _____ _____

4. "蛋糕" 的 "蛋" + "黃色" 的 "黃"

   → 蛋+黃 → _____ _____ _____

5. "天氣熱" 的 "熱" + "狗"

   → 熱+狗 → _____ _____ _____

B. Read the following passage and answer the questions.

　　張英很喜歡日文班的一個男同學。他們是在一個朋友的生日舞會上認識的，他們在一起聊天聊了半個多鐘頭。那個男同學跟張英一樣，是英國人。他的眼睛大大的，鼻子高高的，笑的時候很好看。他又會唱歌又會跳舞。下個星期六學校有個舞會，張英很想請他一起去跳舞，可是不好意思問他。下午下課以後張英回宿舍，和她住在一起的李友說："剛才日文班的一個男的給你打電話，請你下個星期六和他一起去跳舞，可是我忘了他姓什麽了。" 張英聽了以後，有點兒高興，也有點兒緊張，她希望打電話的就是自己喜歡的那位男同學。

Questions (True/False)

( ) 1. 張英喜歡的男孩子是她的朋友的朋友。

( ) 2. 那個男孩子學習日文。

( ) 3. 張英是英國人，可是那個男孩子是日本人。

( ) 4. 張英想請那個男孩子來她家跳舞。

( ) 5. 張英和李友今天上的課是一樣的。

( ) 6. 李友知道打電話的那個人是日文班的學生。

( ) 7. 張英知道請她跳舞的那個人就是她喜歡的那個男孩子。

C. Read the following dialogue and answer the questions.

（在李友的生日舞會上）

李友：哎，王朋，你怎麽現在才來？

王朋：對不起，我來晚了。李友，這是我送給你的生日禮物。

李友：謝謝。

王朋：還有一個禮物。

李友：哎，這是我忘在圖書館的中文書！太好了！你是什麽時候找到的？

王朋：剛找到的。

李友：你是怎麼找到的？

王朋：我有一個朋友，在圖書館工作。他幫我找，我們一
　　　起找了兩個多小時才找到。

李友：在哪兒找到的？

王朋：在日文書那邊。圖書館裏的人不認識中文，他們覺
　　　得中文跟日文一樣。雖然你在書上寫了你的中文名
　　　字，可是他們不認識那兩個字。

李友：王朋，你真好。

Questions (True/False)

( ) **1.** Li You was anxiously awaiting Wang Peng's arrival.

( ) **2.** Wang Peng may have spent at least two hours in the library today.

( ) **3.** Wang Peng spent a lot of money on his second birthday gift for Li You.

( ) **4.** Wang Peng had told Li You that he would look for her lost book.

Questions (Multiple Choice)

( ) **5.** Wang Peng went to look for the book today because _____.

    a. he wanted to make Li You happy on her birthday

    b. he knew his librarian friend was working today

    c. he wanted to save money on a birthday gift

( ) **6.** The librarians hadn't found the book earlier because _____.

    a. Li You didn't write her name on it as she said

    b. they couldn't tell written Chinese from written Japanese

    c. they knew that Wang Peng would find it anyway

D. Read the passage, answer the questions in English, and draw a picture based on the passage.

這是我的狗，他的毛 (máo, hair; fur) 是黑色的，我叫他小
黑。因為我屬狗，所以我爸爸媽媽送小黑給我做生日禮
物。他長得很可愛，臉大大的，嘴小小的，鼻子不高。

我常常帶他到公園去玩。他跟我一樣，也喜歡吃肉，喝飲料，不喜歡運動，每天晚上也睡九個鐘頭的覺。你看，這是小黑的照片，他正在笑呢！

1. What's the dog's name? Who gave him that name, and why?
2. Why did the narrator's parents give her a dog as her birthday gift?
3. What do you know about the narrator from the passage?

E. What does this store sell? What kind of discount does it offer? _____

IV. Writing Exercises

A. Building Characters

Form a character by fitting the given components together as indicated. Then provide a word or phrase in which that character appears.

EXAMPLE: 左邊一個 "女" ，右邊一個 "子"

是 "好久不見" 的 "好" 。

1. 左邊一個 "女" ，右邊一個 "而且" 的 "且" 是
_____ 的 _____ 。

2. 左邊一個 "糸" ，右邊一個 "工作" 的 "工" 是
_____ 的 _____ 。

3. 上邊一個 "日" ，下邊一個 "或者" 的 "者" 是
_____ 的 _____ 。

4. 左邊一個 "工作" 的 "工" ，右邊一個 "力" 是
_____ 的 _____ 。

5. 左邊一個 "目" ，右邊一個 "青菜" 的 "青" 是
_____ 的 _____ 。

B. Your friend is studying apparel merchandising and would like to interview you for a marketing class assignment. Answer the following questions based on what you are wearing today.

1. 你的衣服是什麼時候買的？

_____

2. 你的衣服是在哪兒買的？

_____

3. 你的衣服是誰買的？

_____

4. 你的衣服是花多少錢買的？

_____

C. Answer the following questions based on your own situation.

1. A: 你平常每天做功課做多長時間？

   B: _____。

   A: 昨天呢？

   B: _____。

2. A: 你平常吃晚飯吃多長時間？

   B: _____。

   A: 昨天呢？

   B: _____。

3. A: 你平常洗澡洗多長時間？

   B: _____。

   A: 昨天呢？

   B: _____。

D. Describe the dog in the picture. Include as many details as you can. (PRESENTATIONAL)

E. Describe what you hope your ideal boyfriend/girlfriend would look like. (PRESENTATIONAL)

F. Translate the following into Chinese. (PRESENTATIONAL)

1. **A:** Little Li is a good student. He is smart and hardworking.

    _____

    B: I heard he does homework for four hours every night.

    _____

    A: But he likes to exercise, too. We exercised for an hour yesterday afternoon at the student center.

    _____

    _____

    B: Really? He is quite busy.

    _____

2. **A:** Who's that guy skating?

    _____

    B: That's my boyfriend, Tom.

    _____

    A: He's quite handsome. Is he older or younger than you?

    _____

    B: He's the same age as I am. We were both born in 1990.

    _____

    A: Where did you meet?

    _____

    B: We met in the park.

    _____

3.   The man who is cooking over there is my older brother. My mother used to say that my older brother was smart and hardworking, and that he would be a great lawyer like her after he grew up. But my older brother is not a lawyer. He likes to cook, and the food he makes is extremely good. He now works in a restaurant. He is not like my mother at all.

G. You are planning a birthday party for your best friend. Please write up a plan for the guest of honor to review. The plan needs to include information such as whom you are inviting, where the party takes place, what people can bring to the party, what activities there will be, how long each activity will last, and what gifts your friend might wish to receive. Some of the party guests may need a ride to the party; include suggestions for their travel plans. (PRESENTATIONAL)

H. Storytelling (PRESENTATIONAL)

Write a story in Chinese based on the four cartoons below. Make sure that your story has a beginning, middle, and end. Also make sure that the transition from one picture to the next is smooth and logical.

1

2

3

4

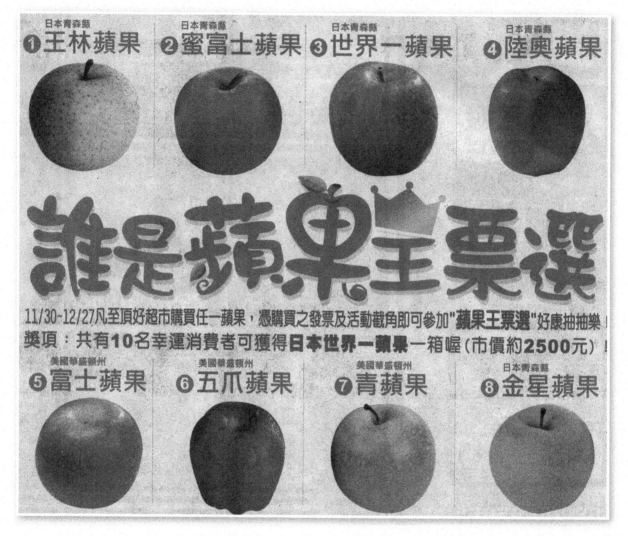

你喜歡吃哪種蘋果？

15

LESSON 15 **Seeing a Doctor**

第十五課 看病

PART ONE Dialogue I: My Stomachache Is Killing Me!

I. Listening Comprehension

A. Textbook Dialogue (Multiple Choice) (INTERPRETIVE)

( ) **1.** Gao Wenzhong has not been feeling well since_____.

    a. last week
    b. five days ago
    c. yesterday morning
    d. last night

( ) **2.** Gao Wenzhong has a stomachache because _____.

    a. he had too much ice
    b. he has an ulcer
    c. he ate some spoiled food
    d. he drank polluted water

( ) **3.** Gao Wenzhong needs to take _____.

    a. three pills twice a day
    b. two pills three times a day
    c. one pill three times a day
    d. two pills twice a day

( ) **4.** The doctor recommends that Gao Wenzhong _____.

    a. abstain from food for twenty-four hours
    b. drink nothing but water for twenty-four hours
    c. rest for twenty-four hours
    d. come back to the clinic in twenty-four hours

B. Workbook Narrative (INTERPRETIVE)

Answer the following questions after listening to the short passage:

1. What is the dog's name? Why do you think it has a name like that?

_____

2. What does the speaker do annually to care for the dog? List two things.

_____

3. What is the good news about the dog?

_____

4. What is the bad news about the dog? List two things.

_____

5. What did the doctor tell the speaker *not* to do?

_____

C. Listening Rejoinder (INTERPERSONAL)

In this section, you will hear two speakers talking. After hearing the first speaker, select the best from the four possible responses given by the second speaker.

_____

II. Speaking Exercises

A. Answer the questions in Chinese based on the Textbook Dialogue. (INTERPRETIVE/PRESENTATIONAL)

1. Why did Gao Wenzhong go to the doctor?

2. How did his symptoms start?

3. What did the doctor say about the cause of his illness?

4. What were the instructions on his prescription?

5. What did the doctor suggest Gao Wenzhong should do in addition to taking the prescription?

B. With a partner, do a role play as a doctor and a patient. The patient describes his/her symptoms and asks the doctor about the treatment. The doctor responds and gives instructions based on the label below. (INTERPERSONAL)

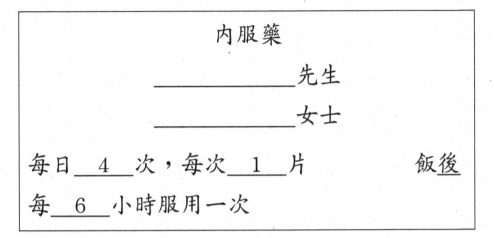

內服藥

＿＿＿＿＿＿＿先生

＿＿＿＿＿＿＿女士

每日＿＿4＿＿次，每次＿1＿片　　　　　飯後

每＿＿6＿＿小時服用一次

III. Reading Comprehension (INTERPRETIVE)

A. Building Words

If you combine the *zhōng* in *Zhōngguó* with the *yī* in *yīshēng*, you have *zhōngyī*, as seen in #1 below. Can you guess what the word *zhōngyī* means? Complete this section by providing the characters, the pinyin, and the English equivalent of each new word formed this way. You may consult a dictionary if necessary.

	new word	*pinyin*	English

1. "中國" 的 "中" + "醫生" 的 "醫"

   → 中+醫 → ＿＿＿＿＿＿　＿＿＿＿＿＿　＿＿＿＿＿＿

2. "東南西北" 的 "西" + "醫生" 的 "醫"

   → 西+醫 → ＿＿＿＿＿＿　＿＿＿＿＿＿　＿＿＿＿＿＿

3. "公共汽車" 的 "公" + "廁所" 的 "廁"

   → 公+廁 → ＿＿＿＿＿＿　＿＿＿＿＿＿　＿＿＿＿＿＿

4. "寫信" 的 "信" + "冰箱" 的 "箱"

   → 信+箱 → ＿＿＿＿＿＿　＿＿＿＿＿＿　＿＿＿＿＿＿

5. "吃藥" 的 "藥" + "檢查" 的 "檢"

   → 藥+檢 → ＿＿＿＿＿＿　＿＿＿＿＿＿　＿＿＿＿＿＿

B. Read the following passage and answer the questions.

因為今天要考試，小黃昨天晚上把功課做完以後就開始看書，今天早上四點才睡覺，六點就起床了。一起床他就覺得頭有一點兒疼。考完試以後，小黃的頭越來越疼，就去看醫生。醫生說小黃沒什麼問題，只是睡覺不夠，今天晚上多睡一點就好了。醫生沒有給他打針，也沒給他藥吃。

Questions (True/False)

( ) **1.** 小黃昨天晚上先做功課，然後看書。

( ) **2.** 因為小黃考試考得不好，所以他頭疼。

( ) **3.** 考試以後，小黃的頭比起床的時候更疼了。

( ) **4.** 醫生覺得小黃的病很重。

( ) **5.** 醫生告訴小黃今天晚上得多睡覺。

( ) **6.** 醫生覺得小黃不用打針，也不用吃藥。

C. Read the following passage and answer the questions.

小錢以前住在學生宿舍，每天在學生餐廳吃飯。餐廳的菜很便宜，可是不好吃，小錢常常吃很少一點東西就不想吃了。小錢的媽媽知道了，就說，"回家來住吧。"這個學期小錢住在家裏，每天都吃媽媽做的菜，覺得好吃極了。小錢家離學校很遠，她每天早上很早就得起床，然後坐地鐵去上課。因為她睡覺睡得不夠，眼睛常常是紅紅的，有點兒不舒服。可是小錢還是覺得住在家裏比住在學生宿舍好。

Questions (True/False):

( ) **1.** Little Qian has been living at home for a year.

( ) **2.** When she lived on campus, Little Qian had to spend a lot of money on food.

( ) **3.** Little Qian's mother is a good cook.

( ) **4.** Little Qian's eyes are often uncomfortable because of some kind of allergy.

( ) **5.** We can assume that Little Qian will not move back to the dorm soon.

D. Read the following passage and answer the questions.

　　李友星期四晚上請王紅教她做了一盤家常豆腐，沒吃完，就把没吃完的豆腐放在冰箱裏了。星期五李友吃早飯，吃了幾口豆腐，上課的時候肚子就疼起來了。李友一下課就去看醫生，醫生檢查了一下，説是吃壞肚子了。李友不懂那盤豆腐在冰箱裏只放了八、九個小時，怎麼會把肚子吃壞了呢？她打電話請王朋來幫她看看冰箱，王朋檢查了以後説："冰箱壞了。"

Questions (True/False)

( ) **1.** Li You cooked a tofu dish and invited Wang Hong to dinner.

( ) **2.** The tofu dish was the cause of Li You's stomachache.

( ) **3.** When Li You went to the doctor, it took the doctor a long time to diagnose the problem.

( ) **4.** Until she saw the doctor, Li You had taken for granted that her refrigerator was functioning properly.

( ) **5.** Li You asked Wang Peng to help her look for a new refrigerator.

E. This is an instruction label on a prescription drug bottle. Explain in Chinese what you think the character *"服"* means.

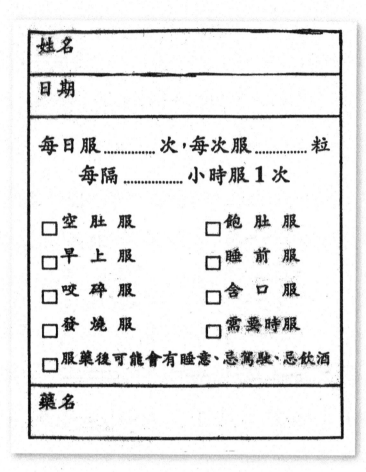

姓名

日期

每日服 .... 次，每次服 .... 粒
每隔 .... 小時服 **1** 次

☐ 空 肚 服   ☐ 飽 肚 服
☐ 早 上 服   ☐ 睡 前 服
☐ 咬 碎 服   ☐ 含 口 服
☐ 發 燒 服   ☐ 需 要 時 服
☐ 服藥後可能會有睡意、忌駕駛、忌飲酒

藥名

_____

IV. Writing Exercises

A. Ask and answer questions based on the illustrations given.

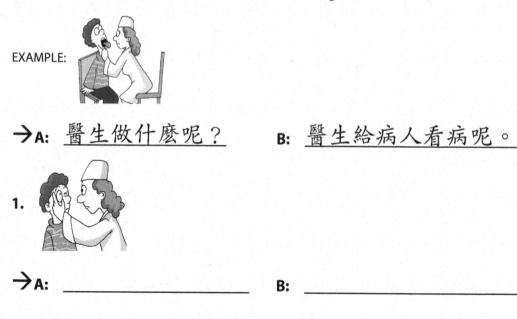

EXAMPLE:

→A: <u>醫生做什麼呢？</u>   B: <u>醫生給病人看病呢。</u>

1.

→A: _____   B: _____

2.

→**A:** _____   **B:** _____

3.

→**A:** _____   **B:** _____

B. Answer the following questions based on your own situation.

1. 你每個星期上幾次中文課？

_____

2. 你每個星期工作幾次？

_____

3. 你每個星期運動幾次？

_____

4. 你每個月洗幾次衣服？

_____

5. 你昨天喝了幾次水？

_____

C. Imagine that your younger brother is coming to stay with you for a few weeks. You need to let him know how to keep the house in order and tell him where he can place his things.

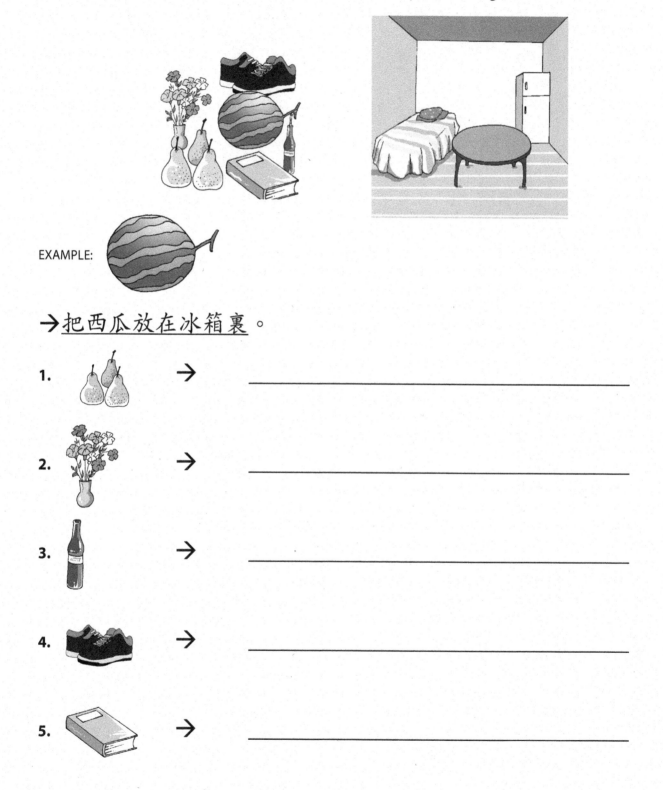

EXAMPLE:

→ 把西瓜放在冰箱裏。

1. → _____

2. → _____

3. → _____

4. → _____

5. → _____

D. What does your teacher often say to the class?

EXAMPLE: Please hand in your homework.   → <u>請把功課給我</u> 。

1. Please finish your homework.   → _____

2. Please finish listening to the audio.   → _____

3. Please write the characters correctly.   → _____

E. Translate the following into Chinese. (PRESENTATIONAL)

1. **A:** Where is the watermelon I bought?

   _____

   B: I put it in the refrigerator.

   _____

2. **A:** I drank three glasses of water before bed last night, and I went to the bathroom twice late last night.

   _____

   B: You'd better not drink any water before bed.

   _____

3. The teacher asked us to listen to the audio recording ten times every day. But I often listen to it three times. Last night, I only listened once. I hope the teacher won't ask me to read the text aloud today. I will definitely do a very bad job.

   _____

   _____

   _____

   _____

PART TWO Dialogue II: Allergies

I. Listening Comprehension

A. Textbook Dialogue (Multiple Choice) (INTERPRETIVE)

( ) **1.** Wang Peng's eyes are red because _____.

    a. they are infected
    b. he is suffering from allergies
    c. he has been crying
    d. he is wearing contact lenses

( ) **2.** Wang Peng has been self-medicating because _____.

    a. he doesn't have health insurance
    b. he is too busy to see a doctor
    c. he has the right medicine
    d. he knows a lot about medicine

( ) **3.** Li You thinks that Wang Peng should _____.

    a. take his illness more seriously
    b. be more careful with his money
    c. not be too reliant on pills
    d. not worry about his health incessantly

( ) **4.** Li You offers to _____.

    a. buy some new medicine for Wang Peng
    b. lend Wang Peng some money for better health insurance
    c. go to the doctor's office with Wang Peng
    d. call a doctor friend for advice

B. Workbook Narrative (True/False) (INTERPRETIVE)

Answer the following questions after listening to the short telephone message:

( ) **1.** The message was left by the caller on her brother's answering machine.
( ) **2.** The caller's mother called today.
( ) **3.** The mother doesn't know that her son is suffering from allergies.
( ) **4.** The caller assumes her brother will seek treatment this morning.
( ) **5.** The caller wants her brother to call their mother.
( ) **6.** The caller would like to see a Chinese film tomorrow.

C. Listening Rejoinder (INTERPERSONAL)

In this section, you will hear two speakers talking. After hearing the first speaker, select the best from the four possible responses given by the second speaker.

_____

II. Speaking Exercises

A. Answer the questions in Chinese based on the Textbook Dialogue. (INTERPRETIVE/PRESENTATIONAL)

1. What are Wang Peng's symptoms?
2. What does Li You think Wang Peng's problem is?
3. Where did Wang Peng get his medication?
4. Why doesn't Wang Peng see a doctor?
5. What does Wang Peng plan to do about his illness?

B. With a partner, discuss what each of you does when you have a cold (such as seeing a doctor, taking medicine, resting and staying home from school or work, or other ways of recuperating). (INTERPERSONAL)

C. With a partner, do a role play. You are feeling ill, but you don't feel like seeing a doctor. Describe your symptoms and explain why you don't want to go to the doctor. Your partner tries his/her best to persuade you to see a doctor. (INTERPERSONAL)

III. Reading Comprehension (INTERPRETIVE)

A. Building Words

If you combine the *bìng* in *shēng bìng* with the *chuáng* in *qǐ chuáng*, you have *bìngchuáng*, as seen in #1 below. Can you guess what the word *bìngchuáng* means together as a word? Complete this section by providing the characters, the *pinyin*, and the English equivalent of each new word formed this way. You may consult a dictionary if necessary.

	new word	pinyin	English

1. "生病" 的 "病" + "起床" 的 "床"

   → 病+床 → _____ _____ _____

2. "生病" 的 "病" + "寒假" 的 "假"

   → 病+假 → _____ _____ _____

3. "身體" 的 "身" + "高"

   → 　身+高　→ ＿＿＿＿＿　＿＿＿＿＿　＿＿＿＿＿

4. "身體" 的 "體" + "檢查" 的 "檢"

   → 　體+檢　→ ＿＿＿＿＿　＿＿＿＿＿　＿＿＿＿＿

5. "身體" 的 "體" + "重"

   　 體+重　→ ＿＿＿＿＿　＿＿＿＿＿　＿＿＿＿＿

B. Read the following passage and answer the questions.

醫生：你哪兒不舒服？

病人：醫生，我肚子疼死了。

醫生：我給你檢查一下。你昨天吃什麼東西了？

病人：我昨天晚上吃了一盤糖醋魚和幾個餃子。

醫生：我知道了，一定是那盤糖醋魚有問題。你得趕快吃
　　　藥，要不然你的肚子會越來越疼。你去的那個飯館
　　　一定很便宜，對不對？你以後出去吃飯，一定要去
　　　貴的飯館。雖然多付一點錢，可是你吃了不會生
　　　病。

病人：您說得對，那家飯館很便宜，可是我覺得那盤魚真
　　　的很好吃，不會有問題。

醫生：你是在哪個飯館吃的？

病人：在我們學校南邊的那家小飯館。

醫生：是嗎？⋯哎，糟糕了！

病人：醫生，您怎麼了？

醫生：我的肚子也疼起來了，昨天晚上我也是在那家飯館
吃的晚飯。

Questions (True/False)

( ) **1.** The patient and the doctor meet in a restaurant.

( ) **2.** The patient has a stomachache.

( ) **3.** Neither the doctor nor the patient had dinner at home yesterday.

( ) **4.** The doctor urges the patient to take medicine as soon as possible.

( ) **5.** The doctor always dines at expensive restaurants.

Questions (Multiple Choice)

( ) **6.** What is the doctor's logic as he tries to diagnose the patient's problem?

  a. If the food was the problem, the restaurant must have been cheap.

  b. If the patient got a stomachache, he must have eaten spoiled fish.

  c. If a restaurant is cheap, it must have served cheap fish dishes.

( ) **7.** What is the doctor's advice to the patient about dining out?

  a. Go to more expensive restaurants where the food is tastier.

  b. Go to more reputable restaurants where the food is more expensive.

  c. Go to more expensive restaurants where the food is safer.

( ) **8.** What can we say about the doctor?

  a. He himself follows the advice he gives to his patient.

  b. He himself does not follow the advice he gives to his patient.

  c. He advises his patient to do things his way.

C. Read the following passage and answer the questions.

　　小高這幾天一直不舒服。上個週末他頭疼，醫生給了
他一些藥，他吃了兩次就好了。可是星期一小高覺得鼻子
很癢，眼睛紅紅的。醫生說他一定是對什麼過敏了。醫生
給了他一種藥，可是小高吃了三天，一點兒用也沒有。今
天上午小高又去看醫生，想請醫生給點兒別的藥試試。醫

生請他把他吃的藥拿出來看看，才知道小高這幾天吃的不是過敏藥，是頭疼藥！

Questions (True/False)

( ) **1.** 小高上個週末和這個星期都不太舒服。

( ) **2.** 小高吃了頭疼藥，頭很快就不疼了。

( ) **3.** 上個星期天小高把頭疼藥都吃完了。

( ) **4.** 醫生說，小高對頭疼藥過敏，所以眼睛紅紅的。

( ) **5.** 星期三小高的眼睛不紅了，鼻子也不癢了。

( ) **6.** 小高今天上午又去看醫生，因為他覺得醫生給他的過敏藥沒有用。

( ) **7.** 因為小高吃錯藥了，所以他的病還沒好。

D. Read the following passage and answer the questions.

　　李友的朋友小錢很喜歡學校醫院的一位男醫生。小錢身體很健康，可是為了去看那位醫生，就說自己鼻子癢，眼睛疼，一定是對什麼過敏了。李友一邊笑一邊說："你平常不過敏，怎麼一看到那位長得很帥的男醫生眼睛就疼起來，鼻子就癢起來了？你一定是對那位醫生過敏了。"

Questions (True/False)

( ) **1.** Little Qian first met the doctor when she went to the hospital for her allergy.

( ) **2.** According to Li You, Little Qian has suffered from her allergy for a long time.

( ) **3.** According to Li You, her allergy is Little Qian's excuse for visiting that doctor.

( ) **4.** Li You knows Little Qian very well.

( ) **5.** Little Qian's allergy symptoms become worse when she sees the doctor.

( ) **6.** Li You suggests that Little Qian should see a different doctor.

E. This is a form that a new patient needs to fill out. Locate the area asking if the patient has any allergic reactions to any drugs.

科　　別：☐內☐婦☐傷☐針灸科 ☐其他				病歷號碼＿＿＿＿＿	

初診日期：　年　　月　　日　　　　☐二年以上未至本院看診　☐健保☐自費

姓　　名		身份證字號		姓別	☐男☐女
出生日期		電話號碼		職業	
出 生 地		手機號碼		血型	
地　　址					
教育程度	☐無　　☐小學　　☐國中　☐高中　☐大學　　☐大學以上				
婚姻狀況	☐未婚　　☐已婚　　☐離婚　　☐寡				
個 人 史	飲食習慣：☐素食☐辛辣☐冷飲☐溫熱食品☐烤炸食品☐外食☐無特殊嗜好 過敏：☐無 ☐藥物＿＿＿＿＿＿＿＿＿ ;☐食物＿＿＿＿＿＿＿ 抽煙：☐無 ☐有　包/天　年。喝酒：☐無☐有　瓶/天，　年（酒類＿＿＿）				
家族病史	☐糖尿病＿＿ ☐高血壓＿＿＿ ☐心臟病＿＿＿ ☐腎臟病＿＿＿ ☐異位性皮膚炎＿＿ ☐中　風＿＿ ☐癌　症＿＿＿ ☐氣　喘＿＿＿ ☐鼻過敏＿＿＿ ☐＿＿＿＿＿＿＿				

IV. Writing Exercises

A. Building Characters

Form a character by fitting the given components together as indicated. Then provide a word or phrase in which that character appears.

EXAMPLE: 外邊一個 "囗"，裏邊一個 "口" 是 <u>回家</u> 的 <u>回</u>。

1. 左邊一個 "月"，右邊一個 "土" 是＿＿＿＿的＿＿＿＿。

2. 外邊一個 "疒"，裏邊一個 "冬天" 的 "冬" 是＿＿＿＿ 的＿＿＿＿。

3. 左邊一個 "金"，右邊一個 "十" 是＿＿＿＿的＿＿＿＿。

4. 左邊一個人字旁，右邊一個 "木" 是＿＿＿＿的＿＿＿＿。

5. 上邊一個 "自己" 的 "自"，下邊一個 "中心" 的

   "心" 是＿＿＿＿的＿＿＿＿。

B. In Chinese, list possible symptoms of the following sicknesses.

1. 感冒：＿＿＿＿＿＿＿＿＿＿＿＿＿＿＿＿＿＿＿＿＿＿＿＿＿＿＿

2. 過敏：＿＿＿＿＿＿＿＿＿＿＿＿＿＿＿＿＿＿＿＿＿＿＿＿＿＿＿

3. 拉 (lā) 肚子 (diarrhea)：＿＿＿＿＿＿＿＿＿＿＿＿＿＿＿＿＿＿

C. Explain in Chinese what each person is allergic to, based on the illustrations given.

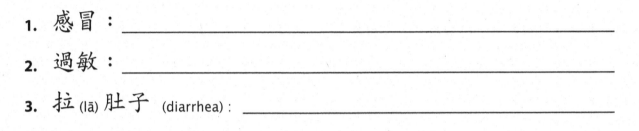

EXAMPLE:

→高文中對味精過敏。

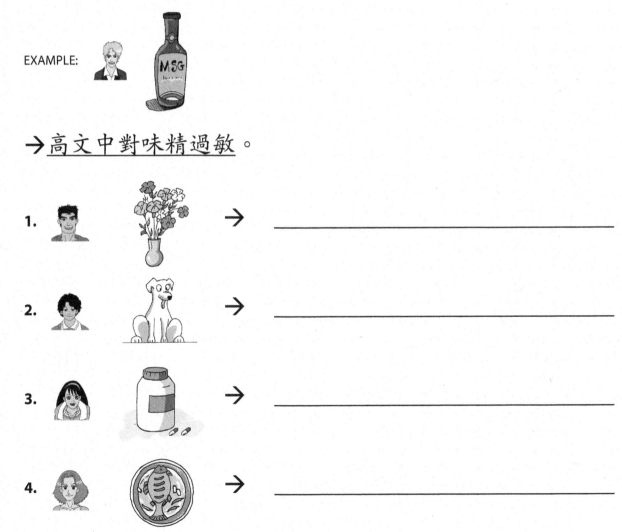

1. → ＿＿＿＿＿＿＿＿＿＿＿＿＿＿＿＿＿＿＿＿

2. → ＿＿＿＿＿＿＿＿＿＿＿＿＿＿＿＿＿＿＿＿

3. → ＿＿＿＿＿＿＿＿＿＿＿＿＿＿＿＿＿＿＿＿

4. → ＿＿＿＿＿＿＿＿＿＿＿＿＿＿＿＿＿＿＿＿

D. Answer the following questions based on your own situation.

1. 最近天氣越來越冷還是越來越暖和？

   _____

2. 你的功課越來越多還是越來越少？

   _____

3. 健康保險越來越貴還是越來越便宜？

   _____

4. 找工作越來越容易還是越來越難？

   _____

E. Translate the following into Chinese. (PRESENTATIONAL)

1. **A:** Do you have a fever?

   _____

   B: I do, but I bought some medicine.

   _____

   A: You can't just take any kind of medicine when you have a fever. You'd better see the doctor.

   _____

   _____

2. **A:** Take out the clothes you bought so I can take a look.

   _____

   B: Here they are.

   _____

A: Why did you buy these clothes?

_____

B: Because they fit well, and besides, they were cheap, too.

_____

3.   **A:**   What's the matter with you? Do you have a cold?

_____

B: My eyes are itchy. I think I am allergic to your dog.

_____

A: But you've been to my house five or six times…

_____

B: My eyes are getting itchier and itchier. Please hurry and give me a ride to see the doctor.

_____

A: I'll give you a ride if you have health insurance. Otherwise, how about having a little lie-down after you take this medicine that my doctor gave me?

_____

_____

F. Storytelling (PRESENTATIONAL)

Write a story in Chinese based on the four cartoons below. Make sure that your story has a beginning, middle and end. Also make sure that the transition from one picture to the next is smooth and logical.

R1 Let's Review (LESSONS 11–15)

I. How do we say these words/phrases?

Write down their correct pronunciation and tones in *pinyin*, and use a tape recorder or computer to record them. Hand in the recording to your teacher if asked.

1. 出去　　去年　　　　＿＿＿＿＿＿　＿＿＿＿＿＿

2. 下雪　　下雨　　　　＿＿＿＿＿＿　＿＿＿＿＿＿

3. 預報　　運動　　　　＿＿＿＿＿＿　＿＿＿＿＿＿

4. 肚子　　舞會　　　　＿＿＿＿＿＿　＿＿＿＿＿＿

5. 路口　　暑期班　　　＿＿＿＿＿＿　＿＿＿＿＿＿

6. 糖醋魚　紅綠燈　　　＿＿＿＿＿＿　＿＿＿＿＿＿

7. 牛肉　　水果　　　　＿＿＿＿＿＿　＿＿＿＿＿＿

8. 遠近　　越來越亂　　我約你＿＿＿＿＿＿　＿＿＿＿＿　＿＿＿＿＿

9. 不餓　　不渴　　　　廁所　　＿＿＿＿＿＿　＿＿＿＿＿　＿＿＿＿＿

10. 樓下　　菜夠了　　　我屬狗　＿＿＿＿＿＿　＿＿＿＿＿　＿＿＿＿＿

11. 長短　　長大　　　　＿＿＿＿＿＿　＿＿＿＿＿＿

12. 覺得　　睡覺　　　　＿＿＿＿＿＿　＿＿＿＿＿＿

II. Group the characters according to their radicals, and provide the meaning of each radical.

肚　暖　冷　網　桌　素　熱
碟　醋　餓　暑　疼　冰　餃　約　糟　病　酸　糕
碗　精　燈　樓　臉　燒　癢　梨　飲

Radical	Meaning of the Radical (English)	Characters
1. _____	_____	_____
2. _____	_____	_____
3. _____	_____	_____
4. _____	_____	_____
5. _____	_____	_____
6. _____	_____	_____
7. _____	_____	_____
8. _____	_____	_____
9. _____	_____	_____
10. _____	_____	_____
11. _____	_____	_____

III. VO or Not

Among the verbs below, distinguish those that are VO compounds from those that are not.

滑冰   下雪   點菜   檢查

打針   看病   過敏   聽説

VO Compounds: _____

not VO Compounds: _____

IV. Have You Seen that Character Before?

Circle the character shared by the words in each group. Write down the *pinyin* for the character in common, and define the character's original meaning.

		pinyin	meaning
1. 預習	預報	_____	_____
2. 常常	平常 非常 家常豆腐	_____	_____
3. 售貨員	服務員	_____	_____
4. 考試	面試	_____	_____
5. 糟糕	蛋糕	_____	_____
6. 老師	師傅	_____	_____
7. 黃色	黃瓜	_____	_____
8. 黃瓜	西瓜	_____	_____
9. 運動場	活動中心	_____	_____
10. 飛機場	運動場	_____	_____
11. 商店	書店	_____	_____
12. 地圖	圖書館	_____	_____
13. 跳舞	舞會	_____	_____
14. 水果	蘋果	_____	_____

15. 功課　　用功　　　　　　　　　　　_____　_____

16. 醫生　　醫院　　　　　　　　　　　_____　_____

17. 冰茶　　冰箱　　　　　　　　　　　_____　_____

18. 發燒　　紅燒牛肉　　　　　　　　　_____　_____

V. Getting to Know You

Put your Chinese to use. Interview one of your classmates to find out more about him/her. After a brief Q & A session, jot down and organize the information you have gathered, and then present an oral or written report to introduce your classmate to the rest of the class. (INTERPERSONAL/PRESENTATIONAL)

A. Food Preferences and Habits

1. 你平常晚飯能吃幾碗米飯？吃得下兩碗嗎？

2. 你先吃飯再喝湯還是先喝湯再吃飯？

3. 你吃素嗎？

4. 你能不能吃辣的？

5. 要是你很餓，你想吃什麼？

6. 你最愛喝什麼飲料？

7. 你最愛吃什麼水果？

8. 你做飯的時候放不放味精？

9. 你對味精過敏嗎？

10. 要是你在飯館點菜，但是你想吃的菜賣完了，你怎麼辦？

11. 你常常吃壞肚子嗎？

12. 如果肚子疼，你怎麼辦？

. . .

B. Clothing and Fashion

你今天穿的衣服

　是在哪兒買的？

　是什麼時候買的？

　是誰買的？

　是花多少錢買的？

你覺得衣服的大小、顏色、樣子（對你）合適不合適？

…

C. Living Situation and Commute

1. 你的學校在你住的地方的哪一邊？

2. 你的學校離你住的地方遠不遠？

3. 你去過學校的學生活動中心嗎？在圖書館的哪一邊？

4. 你平常幾點去學校上課？今天呢？今天是幾點去學校上課的？

5. 你平常怎麼去學校上課？今天呢？今天是怎麼去學校上課的？

D. Academic Studies

1. 你為什麼上這個學校？

2. 你在這個學校學了多長時間了？

3. 你每個星期上幾次中文課？每次上多長時間？

4. 你會用中文發電子郵件嗎？

5. 你常常上網用中文跟人聊天兒嗎？

E. Dream Date

1. 你希望你的男/女朋友長得怎麼樣？

2. 你希望你的男/女朋友是哪一年生的？屬什麼？

3. 你希望你的男/女朋友比你聰明、比你酷嗎？

4. 如果你想約你的男/女朋友出去玩兒，你們會去什麼地方？

16 LESSON 16 Dating
第十六課 約會

PART ONE **Dialogue I: Seeing a Movie**

I. Listening Comprehension

A. Textbook Dialogue (True/False) (INTERPRETIVE)

( ) **1.** Wang Peng and Li You have known each other for almost six months.

( ) **2.** There is a Chinese film at school tonight.

( ) **3.** Wang Peng will have a difficult time getting tickets to the film.

( ) **4.** Li You has seen many Chinese films before.

( ) **5.** Wang Peng and Li You will be going to the film with friends.

B. Workbook Conversation (INTERPRETIVE)

Answer the following questions after listening to the conversation:

1. What does the man offer to do? List four things.

   a. _____

   b. _____

   c. _____

   d. _____

2. What are the four reasons that the woman gives for not accepting the man's invitations and offers?

   a. _____

   b. _____

c. _____

d. _____

3. What does the woman really want?

_____

4. Does the man get the message?

_____

C. Listening Rejoinder (INTERPERSONAL)

In this section, you will hear two speakers talking. After hearing the first speaker, select the best from the four possible responses given by the second speaker.

_____

II. Speaking Exercises

A. Answer the questions in Chinese based on the Textbook Dialogue. (INTERPRETIVE/PRESENTATIONAL)

1. How long have Li You and Wang Peng known each other?

2. How did Li You and Wang Peng become good friends?

3. What would Wang Peng like to invite Li You to do this weekend?

4. Was it easy for Wang Peng to get tickets? Why or why not?

5. What additional plans have Wang Peng and Li You made for the day of the event?

B. With a partner, do a role play. Invite your partner to go to the movies with you this weekend. Decide together which movie you should see, and discuss what you could do before and after the movie. (INTERPERSONAL)

C. My Best Friend: Tell your classmates how you met your best friend, how long you have known each other, why you like him/her, and what you usually do together. (PRESENTATIONAL)

III. Reading Comprehension (INTERPRETIVE)

A. Building Words

If you combine the *tóng* in *tóng yí ge* with the *bān* in *shǔqī bān*, you have *tóngbān*, as seen in #1 below. Can you guess what the word *tóngbān* means? Complete this section by providing the characters, the *pinyin*, and the English equivalent of each new word formed this way. You may consult a dictionary if necessary.

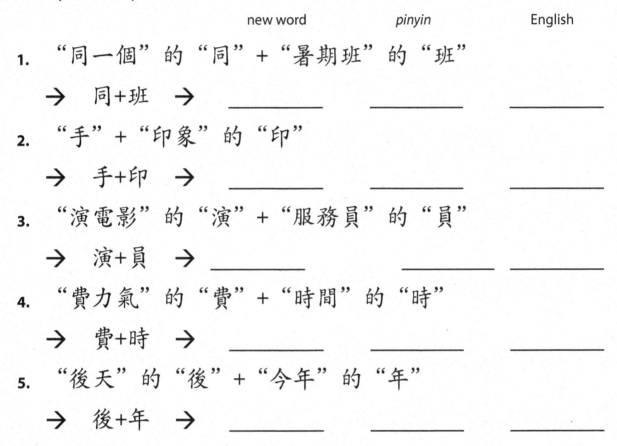

	new word	*pinyin*	English
1. "同一個"的"同" + "暑期班"的"班" → 同+班 →	_____	_____	_____
2. "手" + "印象"的"印" → 手+印 →	_____	_____	_____
3. "演電影"的"演" + "服務員"的"員" → 演+員 →	_____	_____	_____
4. "費力氣"的"費" + "時間"的"時" → 費+時 →	_____	_____	_____
5. "後天"的"後" + "今年"的"年" → 後+年 →	_____	_____	_____

B. Read the following passage and answer the questions.

　　小謝跟小黃認識已經快兩年了，他們是英文班的同學。小黃去過英國，英文說得很好，常常幫小謝練習說英文。小黃做飯做得不太好，週末的時候，小謝常常請小黃到她家去吃飯。小黃對小謝的印象越來越好。小謝覺得小黃又聰明，又用功，對他的印象也很好。上個週末小謝的爸爸媽媽來看她，小謝把小黃介紹給爸媽認識。小謝的爸媽覺得小黃長得不錯，學習也不錯，很喜歡小黃。

Questions (True/False)

( ) **1.** 小謝的英文老師也是小黃的英文老師。

( ) **2.** 兩年以前小謝不認識小黃。

( ) **3.** 小謝說英文說得比小黃好。

( ) **4.** 週末小謝常常請小黃到飯館去吃飯。

( ) **5.** 小黃覺得小謝是個很好的女孩子。

( ) **6.** 小謝喜歡小黃，但小謝的爸媽覺得他們在一起不合適。

C. Read the following passage and answer the questions.

　　高文中對白英愛印象很好，可是他不知道白英愛對他印象怎麼樣，所以一直沒有告訴姐姐高小音他喜歡白英愛，朋友們也都不知道。高小音問他喜歡什麼樣的女孩子，文中說："眼睛大大的，鼻子高高的，嘴不大也不小。得聰明，會跳舞，還會做飯。"小音覺得要找到這麼好的女孩子，得費很大力氣。高文中又說："那個女孩子最好姓白。"小音才知道高文中說的一定是白英愛。

Questions:

1. Why hasn't Gao Wenzhong told his sister how he feels about Bai Ying'ai?

_____

2. Do any of Gao Wenzhong's friends know for sure how Gao Wenzhong feels about Bai Ying'ai? Why or why not?

_____

3. What is Gao Wenzhong's "dream girl" like?

_____

4. Was Gao Xiaoyin optimistic at first about her brother's chances of meeting his "dream girl"? Why or why not?

_____

5. Does Gao Xiaoyin now know who Gao Wenzhong's dream girl is? Who is she?

_____

D. Look at the listing and answer the following questions.

❀ 印象電影院
週二全天半價：週一至五 12:00前半價
上映影片：
《危情24小時》　9:00　10:55　12:50
14:45　16:40　18:35
《功夫熊貓》　 9:00　11:50　12:40
13:40　15:30　16:20　17:20　19:10
20:00　20:30　21:00
《精舞門》 10:50　14:30　18:10

1. What's the name of this movie theater? _____

2. How many movies are currently playing in this theater? _____

3. How many showings are there daily for the first movie? _____

4. Can you get a half-price ticket if you go to see a movie in this theater on a Monday morning?_____

IV. Writing Exercises

A. Answer the following questions based on your own situation.

1. **A:** 你去過哪些城市？

   B: _____

   A: 你對哪一個城市的印象最糟糕？

   B: _____

2. **A:** 你去過哪些學校？

   B: _____

   A: 你對哪一個學校的印象最好？

   B: _____

3. **A:** 你看過中國電影嗎？

   B: _____

   A: 你對中國電影的印象怎麼樣？

   B: _____

B. Are the following items available for purchase in the place where you live?

EXAMPLE: 中國音樂

A: 這個城市買得到買不到中國音樂？

B: 這個城市買得到中國音樂。／

這個城市買不到中國音樂。

1. 中國影碟 (movie DVDs)

   A: _____

   B: _____

2. 中國地圖

   A: _____

   B: _____

3. 中國綠茶

   A: _____

   B: _____

C. Are the following dishes available in your local restaurants?

EXAMPLE:　紅燒牛肉

A: <u>這個城市吃得到吃不到紅燒牛肉</u>？

B: <u>這個城市吃得到紅燒牛肉。</u>/
<u>這個城市吃不到紅燒牛肉。</u>

1. 涼拌黃瓜

   A: _____

   B: _____

2. 糖醋魚

A: _____

B: _____

3. 家常豆腐

A: _____

B: _____

D. You are leaving for a trip tomorrow night and need to figure out whether you can finish the food in your refrigerator before you leave.

Example: 米飯 ✓

A: 冰箱裏的米飯，明天吃得完吃不完？

B: （冰箱裏的米飯，明天）吃得完。

1. 青菜 ✗

A: _____   B: _____

2. 餃子 ✓

A: _____   B: _____

3. 飲料 ✗

A: _____   B: _____

4. 湯 ✓

A: _____   B: _____

E. Translate the following exchanges into Chinese. (PRESENTATIONAL)

1. **A:** There are six pears on the table. Would you like to eat some?

    _____

    B: I can't eat pears. I am allergic to them.

    _____

    C: I can eat them. But six pears are too many. I can't eat them all.

    _____

2. **A:** I made three hundred dumplings yesterday. It took me a lot of effort to get the dumplings ready.

    _____

    B: How many people were making the dumplings?

    _____

    A: Only me, one person.

    _____

3. **A:** I have a great impression of Beijing. I would like to go there again.

    _____

    B: Great! I've always wanted to go to Beijing. But would we be able to get airline tickets?

    _____

    A: We have to hurry. Otherwise, it's possible that we won't be able to get them.

    _____

F. Provide a brief history of your friendship with someone, including who your friend is, when and where you met, how long you have known each other, when you became friends, what your friend does well, what attributes your friend has, what he/she looks like, what you have in common, what you often do together, etc. (PRESENTATIONAL)

PART TWO   Dialogue II: Turning Down an Invitation

I. Listening Comprehension

A. Textbook Dialogue (True/False) (INTERPRETIVE)

( ) **1.** Li You recognizes the caller's voice right away.

( ) **2.** Li You is not happy to get the call.

( ) **3.** Li You has never met the caller before.

( ) **4.** The caller wants to ask Li You to go out dancing with him.

( ) **5.** Li You tries to turn the caller down without directly saying so.

B. Workbook Telephone Message (INTERPRETIVE/PRESENTATIONAL)

You accidentally erased a phone message for your roommate. Reconstruct the message from memory and leave a written note in Chinese for your roommate. Take care to note the following information:

Roommate's name   Caller's name
Purpose of the call   Time of the event
Place of the event   Special request

Written message:

_____

_____

_____

_____

C. Listening Rejoinder (INTERPERSONAL)

In this section, you will hear two speakers talking. After hearing the first speaker, select the best from the four possible responses given by the second speaker.

_____

II. Speaking Exercises

A. Answer the questions in Chinese based on the Textbook Dialogue. (INTERPRETIVE/PRESENTATIONAL)

1. According to the caller, when, where, and how did he meet Li You?
2. How did he get Li You's phone number?
3. What was the purpose of his phone call?
4. What is Li You planning to do over the next three weekends?
5. How did Li You end the conversation?

B. With a partner, do a role play. One person should invite the other person to do something with him/her. The second person should come up with different reasons to turn down the invitation. Both parties should be persistent but polite. (INTERPERSONAL)

III. Reading Comprehension (INTERPRETIVE)

A. Building Words

If you combine the *wèn* in *wèntí* with the *hào* in *hàomǎ*, you have *wènhào*, as seen in #1 below. Can you guess what the word *wènhào* means? Complete this section by providing the characters, the *pinyin*, and the English equivalent of each new word formed this way. You may consult a dictionary if necessary.

		new word	*pinyin*	English
1.	"問題" 的 "問" + "號碼" 的 "號"			
	→ 問+號 → _____		_____	_____
2.	"搬出去" 的 "搬" + "我家" 的 "家"			
	→ 搬+家 → _____		_____	_____
3.	"吃藥" 的 "藥" + "房間" 的 "房"			
	→ 藥+房 → _____		_____	_____
4.	"旅行" 的 "旅" + "圖書館" 的 "館"			
	→ 旅+館 → _____		_____	_____
5.	"水電" 的 "電" + "紅綠燈" 的 "燈"			
	→ 電+燈 → _____		_____	_____

B. Read the following passage and answer the questions.

李友：王朋，今天晚上想不想跟我去看電影？我請客。

王朋：看電影？

李友：對，很好看的電影，很多人想看，票我已經買好了。

王朋：你沒有車，票是怎麼買的？

李友：是剛才坐公共汽車去買的。我昨天考試考得不錯，我們好好兒玩兒玩兒吧。

王朋：可是我今天還沒打球呢。

李友：我知道你今天晚上想打球，明天再打吧。

王朋：好，沒問題，我和你去看電影。幾點？

李友：八點…還是八點一刻？讓我看看電影票…糟糕，我把電影票忘在公共汽車上了！

Questions (True/False)

( )**1.** Li You wants to go see a movie because she did well on her exam.
( )**2.** Wang Peng accepts the invitation promptly.
( )**3.** Wang Peng had previously planned to play ball this evening.
( )**4.** We can assume that the movie theater will be half empty this evening.
( )**5.** It is not clear from the tickets whether the movie starts at 8:00 or 8:15.
( )**6.** Li You says that she found the movie tickets on the bus.

C. Read the following dialogue and answer the questions.

高文中：哎，李友，好久不見。明天有一個音樂會，我買了兩張票。一起去聽，好嗎？

李友：　你真客氣，可是，對不起，我明天晚上得整理房間，把我的新買的冰箱搬進來。你還是跟白英愛去吧。

高文中：你不是很喜歡音樂嗎？上個月學校開音樂會，你早上七點鐘就去買票，費了很大力氣才買到，對不對？

李友：　對，我很喜歡聽音樂，可是我明天沒空兒。

高文中：哎，告訴你吧，李友，這兩張票是我幫王朋買的。怎麼樣，明天晚上不想打掃房間了吧？

Questions (True/False)

( ) 1. 李友說明天晚上的音樂會沒有意思。

( ) 2. 王朋找高文中幫他和李友買兩張票，可是沒有告訴李友。

( ) 3. 高文中今天早上七點就去買票了。

( ) 4. 李友說她剛買了一個冰箱，可是冰箱現在不在她的房間裏。

( ) 5. 李友上個月去聽學校的音樂會了。

( ) 6. 上個月學校開音樂會，很多人不想去。

( ) 7. 高文中覺得李友明天晚上不會在家打掃房間，她會跟王朋去聽音樂會。

D. What does the store sell? Please list three items.

_____

_____

_____

IV. Writing Exercises

A. Building Characters

Form a character by fitting the given components together as indicated. Then provide a word or phrase in which that character appears.

EXAMPLE:　上邊一個 "田"，下邊一個 "力氣" 的 "力" 是

　　　<u>"男朋友"</u> 的 <u>"男"</u>。

1.　左邊一個人字旁，右邊一個 "兩個" 的 "兩"

　　是＿＿＿＿＿ 的 ＿＿＿。

2.　左邊一個 "言"，右邊一個 "自己" 的 "己"

　　是＿＿＿＿＿ 的 ＿＿＿。

3.　左邊一個 "走"，右邊一個 "自己" 的 "己"

　　是＿＿＿＿＿的 ＿＿＿。

4.　左邊一個 "石"，右邊一個 "馬" 是＿＿＿＿＿

　　的 ＿＿＿。

5.　上邊一個 "生日" 的 "日"，下邊一個 "醫生"

　　的 "生" 是＿＿＿＿＿的 ＿＿＿。

B. Answer the following questions based on your own situation.

1. **A:** 你記得不記得你上個星期五吃了些什麼東西？

   B: _____ 。

2. **A:** 你想得起來想不起來你中學英文老師叫什麼名字？

   B: _____ 。

3. **A:** 你知道不知道你爸爸、媽媽的手機號碼？

   B: _____ 。

C. An animal obedience trainer is going to China to help Chinese clients train their dogs. The dogs there only understand Chinese. The trainer needs your help to learn some Chinese before his trip. Write down the proper commands in Chinese based on each picture.

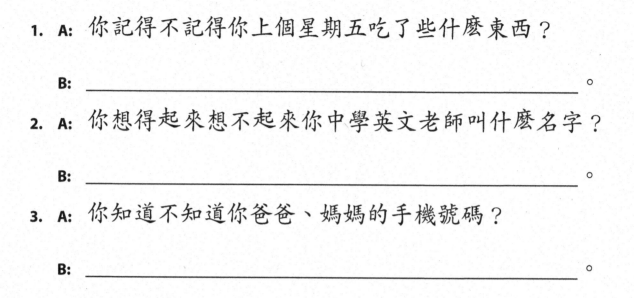

1. _____   2. _____   3. _____   4. _____

5. _____   6. _____   7. _____   8. _____

D. Instruct the movers to move the furniture out of the room based on the illustrations.

EXAMPLE:

→ <u>請把椅子(yǐzi)搬出房間去。/請把椅子(yǐzi)從房間搬出去。</u>

1. 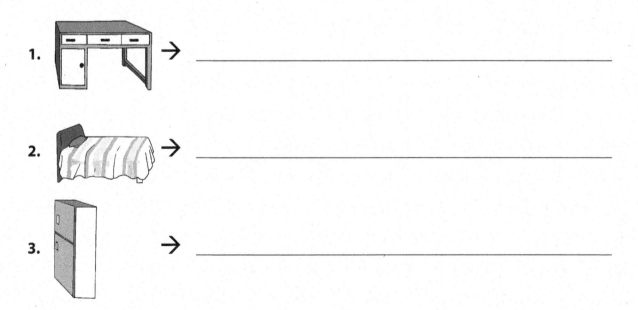 → _____

2. → _____

3. → _____

E. Translate the following into Chinese. (PRESENTATIONAL)

1. **A:** When did you move out of the dorm?

   _____

   B: I moved out in February.

   _____

2. **A:** Who's the woman sitting next to Little Wang? I can't recall.

   _____

   B: I don't know her. I have never met her before.

   _____

3. **A:** I am going to be traveling for a year. Please remember to clean the house once a week.

   _____

   B: No problem. I won't forget. Have fun. Call my cell phone if you need anything.

   _____

F. List three lines that you could use if you need to end a phone conversation without hurting the other person's feelings.

1. _____

2. _____

3. _____

G. List three ways to decline a date indirectly and politely.

1. _____

2. _____

3. _____

H. Describe your perfect date, including the time, the location, and the activity. (PRESENTATIONAL)

I. Storytelling (PRESENTATIONAL)

Write a story in Chinese based on the four cartoons below. Make sure that your story has a beginning, middle and end. Also make sure that the transition from one picture to the next is smooth and logical.

LESSON 17　Renting an Apartment
第十七課 租房子

| PART ONE | Narrative: Finding a Better Place |

I. Listening Comprehension

A. Textbook Narrative (Multiple Choice) (INTERPRETIVE)

( )　**1.** How long has Wang Peng been living in his dorm?

a. two weeks
b. two years
c. two semesters
d. two months

( )　**2.** One thing about his current dorm that does *not* bother Wang Peng is its

a. cost
b. size
c. noise
d. location

( )　**3.** How long has Wang Peng been looking for an apartment?

a. about a week
b. about a month
c. about a year
d. about a semester

( )　**4.** How many rooms does the apartment have?

a. three
b. five
c. four
d. two

B. Workbook Narrative (INTERPRETIVE/INTERPERSONAL)

When Wang Peng returned to the dorm room, he found a new message on his answering machine. Listen to the message and answer the questions.

Questions (True/False)

    ( ) **1.** The speaker is probably a friend of Wang Peng's.

    ( ) **2.** The speaker thinks that he and Wang Peng would be good roommates.

    ( ) **3.** The speaker would like to move off campus.

    ( ) **4.** The speaker is trying to persuade Wang Peng to move into a different dorm.

    ( ) **5.** The speaker thinks it's great to be able to cook for oneself.

Reply to the caller by email on Wang Peng's behalf:

_____

_____

_____

C. Listening Rejoinder (INTERPERSONAL)

In this section, you will hear two speakers talking. After hearing the first speaker, select the best from the four possible responses given by the second speaker.

_____

II. Speaking Exercises (INTERPRETIVE/PRESENTATIONAL)

A. Answer the questions in Chinese based on the Textbook Narrative.

1. Why did Wang Peng want to move out of his dormitory?
2. How long has he been looking for an apartment?
3. How far away from school was the apartment listed in the advertisement he saw?
4. What information did the ad include in addition to the apartment's location?

B. Ask your partner where he/she lives, how far it is away from school, whether he/she likes his/her current place, and why or why not. (INTERPERSONAL)

C. This is Little Xia's place. With a partner, talk about the rooms in the apartment and the furniture in each room. (INTERPERSONAL)

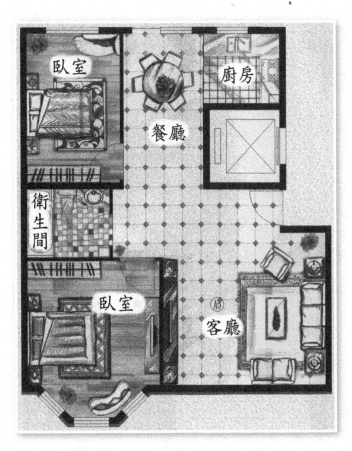

III. Reading Comprehension (INTERPRETIVE)

A. Building Words

If you combine the *wǎn* in *wǎnshang* with the *bào* in *bàozhǐ*, you have *wǎnbào*, as seen in #1 below. Can you guess what the word *wǎnbào* means? Complete this section by providing the characters, the *pinyin*, and the English equivalent of each new word formed this way. You may consult a dictionary if necessary.

		new word	*pinyin*	English
1.	"晚上"的"晚"+"報紙"的"報" → 晚+報 →	_____	_____	_____
2.	"寫信"的"信"+"一張紙"的"紙" → 信+紙 →	_____	_____	_____
3.	"一套"的"套"+"房間"的"間" → 套+間 →	_____	_____	_____

4. "衛生間"的"衛生" + "一張紙"的"紙"

    → 衛生+紙 → ＿＿＿＿＿＿ ＿＿＿＿＿＿ ＿＿＿＿＿＿

5. "廚房"的"廚" + "傢具"的"具"

    → 廚+具 → ＿＿＿＿＿＿ ＿＿＿＿＿＿ ＿＿＿＿＿＿

B. Read the following passage and answer the questions.

　　小馬在學生宿舍住了兩個學期了。因為他的房間很小，放不下兩張床，所以他一個人住一個房間。宿舍裏有餐廳、圖書室、電腦室，還有洗衣房，非常方便。小馬不太會做飯，又很喜歡認識新朋友，所以他覺得住宿舍對他很合適。他聽說在校外租房子比住宿舍便宜，但是得跟別人一起住，還得自己做飯，所以他現在還不知道他下個學期要不要搬出去住。

Questions (True/False)

( ) 1. 小馬是兩個學期以前搬進學生宿舍的。

( ) 2. 雖然房間裏有兩張床，可是沒有別人住在小馬的房間裏。

( ) 3. 小馬想用電腦的時候，得去學校的電腦中心。

( ) 4. 小馬覺得自己做飯沒有在餐廳吃飯方便。

( ) 5. 住學校宿舍雖然比住在學校外邊貴，可是很方便。

( ) 6. 小馬還不清楚他下個學期要住在哪兒。

C. Read the following passage and answer the questions.

　　我是今年寒假搬進我現在住的公寓的。公寓離學校很近，開車只要五分鐘，買東西也很方便。雖然臥室不太大，可是廚房和客廳都很漂亮，而且傢具都是新的，每個月只要五百塊錢。公寓這麼好，怎麼這麼便宜呢？我想這個問題想了三個月，上個星期才聽說很多住過這個公寓的人都生病，而且如果住的時間長，病就會越來越重，不過一搬出這個公寓，他們的病就好了，所以這兒的房租一定得便宜，要不然沒有人住。我應該怎麼辦呢？雖然現在我的身體很健康，可是我得好好兒想想，要不要準備搬家呢？

Questions (True/False)

( ) **1.** The narrator's apartment is inexpensive and conveniently located.

( ) **2.** All of the rooms in the apartment are spacious and beautifully furnished.

( ) **3.** Similar apartments elsewhere in this city are considerably more expensive.

( ) **4.** Before the narrator moved into the apartment, he talked to many former tenants of this apartment building.

Questions (Multiple Choice)

( ) **5.** What happened to many of the people who once lived in this apartment building?

  a. They couldn't find doctors when they got sick.

  b. They couldn't move out when they got sick.

  c. Their health was temporarily affected.

  d. Their health was permanently affected.

( ) **6.** The narrator didn't find out the truth behind the low rent until _____.

  a. winter break

  b. last week

  c. three months ago

  d. March

( ) **7.** The narrator sounds very _____ at the end of the passage.

  a. bitter

  b. ill

  c. indifferent

  d. hesitant

D. Look at the floor plan and answer the following questions.

1. 請用英文寫出這個公寓有什麼房間：

   _____

2. "主臥室"英文是 _____

IV. Writing Exercises

A. What rooms does your apartment, house, or dorm have? List them in Chinese.

_____   _____   _____   _____

                                                                                    . . .

_____   _____   _____   _____

B. Answer the following questions about your living quarters in Chinese.

1. 你住的地方是宿舍、房子、還是公寓？吵不吵？

   _____

2. 你自己一個人住還是跟別人一起住？

   _____

3. 你住的地方帶不帶傢具？

   _____

4. 有沒有自己的廁所、衛生間？

   _____

5. 有沒有廚房？可以做飯嗎？

   _____

6. 上學、坐車、買東西方便不方便？

   _____

7. 附近有什麼飯館、商店？

   _____

8. 臥室大不大？放得下放不下一個大電視？

   _____

9. 你在現在住的地方住了多長時間了？

   _____

10. 下個學期你準備搬家嗎？為什麼？

   _____

C. Answer the following questions about your commute in Chinese.

1. 你今天是怎麼去學校的？走路、開車、還是坐車？

2. 你今天是什麼時候到學校的？

3. 你今天是自己一個人還是跟同學一起去學校的？

4. 你住的地方離學校遠不遠？走路走多長時間？/開車開多長時間？/坐公共汽車坐多長時間？

D. The main cast members of *Integrated Chinese* are all learning something. Ask and answer questions about their new endeavors based on the information given.

EXAMPLE:　　　　　cooking　　　　three months

A: 王朋學做飯學了多長時間了？

B: 王朋學做飯學了三個月了。

1.　　　driving　　　one month

A: _____

B: _____

2.　　　English　　　half a year

A: _____

B: _____

3.　　　ice skating　　　two weeks

A: _____

B: _____

4.　　　computer　　　five days

A: _____

B: _____

E. Describe how much you can eat.

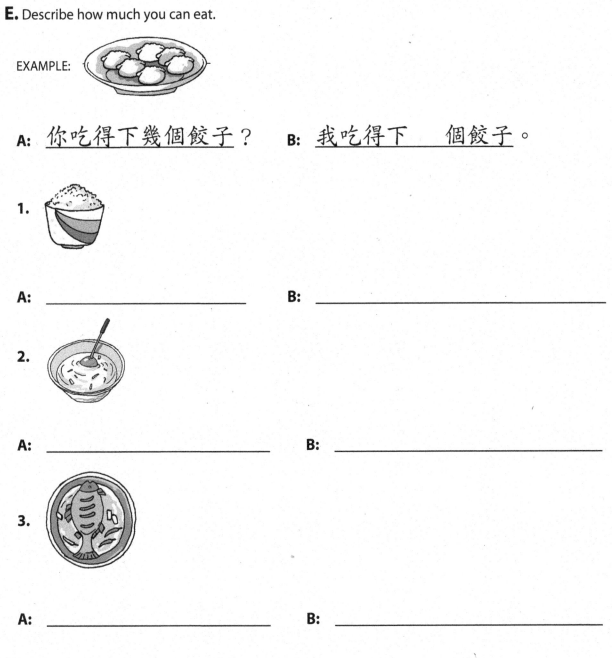

EXAMPLE:

A: 你吃得下幾個餃子？   B: 我吃得下　　個餃子。

1.

A: _____   B: _____

2.

A: _____   B: _____

3.

A: _____   B: _____

F. Translate the following into Chinese. (PRESENTATIONAL)

1. **A:** My apartment is very big. There's enough room for four people.

   _____

   B: My room is small; it can't even fit a big bed.

   _____

2. **A:** The place where I live is close to the stores. It's convenient to go shopping.

_____

B: Is that right? How long does it take to walk to the stores?

_____

A: It only takes three minutes to walk there.

_____

3. **A:** You've been living here for a little over a month. How do you feel?

_____

B: I would like to move out.

_____

A: What's the matter?

_____

B: It's too noisy. I can't get a good night's sleep.

_____

Dialogue: Calling about an Apartment for Rent

PART TWO

I. Listening Comprehension

A. Textbook Dialogue (True/False) (INTERPRETIVE)

( ) **1.** There isn't any furniture in the living room.

( ) **2.** Wang Peng thinks the apartment is a little expensive.

( ) **3.** There do not seem to be any chairs in the bedroom.

( ) **4.** Wang Peng will most likely study in the living room.

( ) **5.** Wang Peng won't have to pay for utilities.

( ) **6.** Wang Peng's first payment will be $1,600.

B. Workbook Narrative (Multiple Choice) (INTERPRETIVE)

( ) **1.** Little Huang's apartment is not very

    a. expensive.
    b. convenient.
    c. noisy.
    d. large.

( ) **2.** Little Huang probably has a

    a. three-room apartment.
    b. studio apartment.
    c. four-room apartment.
    d. two-room apartment.

( ) **3.** Little Huang doesn't have a

    a. bed.
    b. desk.
    c. chair.
    d. bookcase.

( ) **4.** Little Huang wishes his apartment were less

    a. expensive.
    b. noisy.
    c. cramped.
    d. distant from work.

C. Workbook Dialogue (True/False) (INTERPRETIVE)

Questions (True/False)

( )**1.** The bedroom is the best room in the apartment.

( )**2.** The man likes the bedroom, because he will spend most of his time in that room.

( )**3.** The room where the man sleeps is well furnished.

( )**4.** We can assume that nobody will be using the desk.

( )**5.** Pets are allowed in this apartment building.

( )**6.** Meimei likes to eat takeout food.

( )**7.** Meimei is like a faithful servant to the man.

D. Listening Rejoinder (INTERPERSONAL)

In this section, you will hear two speakers talking. After hearing the first speaker, select the best from the four possible responses given by the second speaker.

_____

II. Speaking Exercises

A. Answer the questions in Chinese based on the Textbook Dialogue. (INTERPRETIVE/PRESENTATIONAL)

1. What furniture is provided with the apartment?
2. How much is the rent per month?
3. What kind of discount did the landlady offer Wang Peng?
4. How much is the deposit?
5. Do you think that Wang Peng has ever had pets? Why or why not?

B. Do a role play with a partner. You call your partner (a landlord) and ask about an apartment he/she has for rent. Make sure you get all the details about the apartment, such as its distance from school, the number of rooms, furniture, rent, utilities, deposit, policy on pets, etc. Set up an appointment to see the apartment in person. (INTERPERSONAL)

C. Describe your room, apartment, or your parents' house based on a photo or drawing. You can mention the number of rooms, its location and environment, its distance from school, furniture, etc. (PRESENTATIONAL)

III. Reading Comprehension (INTERPRETIVE)

A. Building Words

If you combine the *lěng* in *hěn lěng* with the *jìng* in *ānjìng*, you have *lěngjìng*, as seen in #1 below. Can you guess what the word *lěngjìng* means? Complete this section by providing the characters, the *pinyin*, and the English equivalent of each new word formed this way. You may consult a dictionary if necessary.

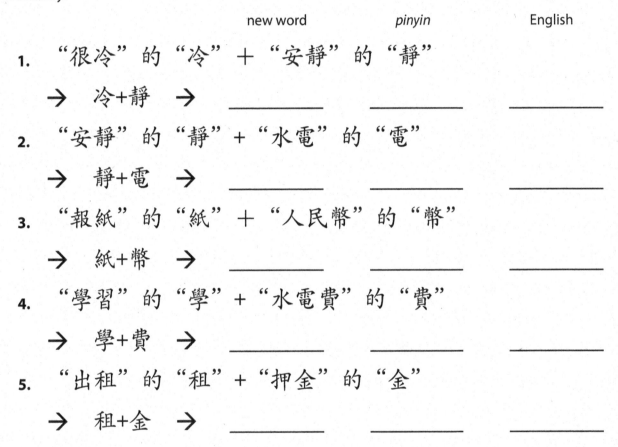

	new word	*pinyin*	English
1. "很冷"的"冷" ＋ "安靜"的"靜"			
→ 冷+靜 →			
2. "安靜"的"靜" ＋ "水電"的"電"			
→ 靜+電 →			
3. "報紙"的"紙" ＋ "人民幣"的"幣"			
→ 紙+幣 →			
4. "學習"的"學" ＋ "水電費"的"費"			
→ 學+費 →			
5. "出租"的"租" ＋ "押金"的"金"			
→ 租+金 →			

B. Read the following passage and answer the questions.

　　小張在學校宿舍住了兩年了，最近才搬出來，在學校附近租了一套公寓，公寓裏什麼傢具都沒有。朋友們告訴小張什麼都不用買，因為他們有很多傢具。他們送給了小張一個書桌，兩個書架和一張床。那張床特別漂亮，哪個傢具店都買不到。他們還說，要是小張還要別的東西，什麼時候給他們打電話都可以。

Questions (True/False)

( ) **1.** Little Zhang has lived in the apartment for two years.

( ) **2.** The apartment is not furnished.

( ) **3.** His friends want to know what furniture Little Zhang wants to buy.

( ) **4.** Little Zhang wonders what furniture store he should visit to find a beautiful bed.

( ) **5.** Little Zhang will not have to spend any money on furniture.

( ) **6.** His friends want to know when Little Zhang will call them.

C. Read the following passage and answer the questions.

小黃上個月在學校附近找了一套小公寓，一房一廳，還帶傢具。房租每個月只要五百二十塊。小黃覺得比住在學校宿舍便宜多了，所以就搬進去了。可是他搬進去以後才知道，他每個月得付九十塊錢的水電費。小黃覺得太貴了。昨天他又找到了一套房子，雖然離學校有一點兒遠，可是很安靜，房租每個月五百四十塊，不用付水電費。小黃對那套公寓很有興趣，想下個星期搬進去。因為他在現在的公寓只住了一個月，所以他得多付一個月的房租才能搬出去。

Questions (True/False)

( ) **1.** Little Huang has lived in his current apartment for one semester.

( ) **2.** Little Huang thought his current apartment was inexpensive when he moved in.

( ) **3.** The student dorm on campus costs $520 per month.

( ) **4.** Little Huang has to pay at least $610 a month for his current apartment.

( ) **5.** Little Huang's current apartment is far away from campus.

( ) **6.** After he moves into the new apartment, he will pay only $540 per month.

( ) **7.** Little Huang's new apartment is quiet but relatively far from campus.

( ) **8.** When he moves out of his current apartment, he will have to pay an extra $90.

D. Draw a picture based on the reading.

　　李先生的家樓下有一個客廳，一個廁所，一個廚房。客廳裏的傢具不多，就一個沙發，一個咖啡桌。你看，李先生正坐在沙發上看報紙呢！廚房裏有一張飯桌和四把椅子。樓上有兩個臥室，一個衛生間。每個臥室都有一張床，李太太正在打掃整理右邊的臥室！左邊的臥室是誰的呢？我想起來了，是他們兒子的房間。他怎麼躺在床上呢？糟糕，他對房子附近的花過敏，眼睛很不舒服！⋯你看，他們家的狗小白正在房子外邊玩呢。小白眼睛大大的，嘴也大大的，非常可愛。

E. Here are two "house for rent" ads. Which of the two would you pick? Why?

IV. Writing Exercises

A. Building Characters

Form a character by fitting the given components together as indicated. Then provide a word or phrase in which that character appears.

EXAMPLE: 上邊一個"田"，下邊一個"力氣"的"力"是 "男朋友"的"男"。

1. 左邊一個"口"，右邊一個"多少"的"少"是 _____ 的 _____ 。

2. 左邊一個"禾"，右邊一個"而且"的"且"是 _____ 的 _____ 。

3. 左邊一個人字旁，右邊一個"寸"是_____ 的 _____ 。

4. 左邊一個三點水，右邊一個"多少"的"少"是 _____ 的 _____ 。

5. 上邊一個"加州"的"加"，下邊一個"木"是 _____ 的 _____ 。

B. List the pieces of furniture in the place where you currently live.

_____   _____   _____   _____

. . .

C. Search online to answer the following questions. Don't forget to cite the website you used and provide the date of your search.

1. 一百元美元能換多少人民幣？→ _____

2. 一百元人民幣能換多少美元？→ _____

網站：_____

日期：_____

D. Rewrite the following sentences.

EXAMPLE: 小夏不認識小王，小白，小張，小高…。

→<u>小夏誰都/也不認識。</u>

1. 老師上午、中午、下午、晚上都沒空。

→_____

2. 這個房間沒有桌子、椅子、床…。

→_____

3. 我弟弟喝茶、喝水、喝可樂、喝咖啡、也喝果汁。

→_____

4. 李老師對小王的印象不好，對小張、小白、小高的印象也不好。

→_____

E. 如果你想租房子，租房子以前，你會問房東哪些問題？

1. _____?

2. _____?

3. _____?

4. _____?

5. _____?

6. _____?

7. _____?

8. _____?

9. _____?

10. _____?

F. 你的朋友正想租房子，下邊是報紙上的一個出租廣告，你覺得對你的朋友很合適。可是你的朋友看不懂英文，請你用中文告訴他廣告上說些什麼。(PRESENTATIONAL)

Apt for Rent

3br, 1LR, 2ba, furnished
quiet

walk to Univ
close to bus stop, shopping, and park
$965 a month, utilities included
no pets allowed

555-5555

G. Translate the following into Chinese. (PRESENTATIONAL)

1. **A:** This living room is so clean.

   _____

   B: It's too clean! It has nothing [in it], not even a piece of furniture or a piece of paper.

   _____

2. **A:** What are you interested in?

   _____

   B: I am interested in keeping pets.

   _____

3.   I've been living with my friend for more than two years. Our apartment is furnished and very close to school, the park, and the bus stop. The rent is less expensive than living in the dorm. I like where I live. My friend is also very nice to me. He cleans the house once a week and often hosts dance parties. Even my mother likes the place I live in. But I may have to move out next semester. It's not because it's so noisy that I cannot sleep well, and it's not because I am allergic to my friend's dog. It's because my friend's cousin is moving in and the place is too small to house three people. It's difficult to find a suitable and affordable apartment. I'm thinking I could ask my friend if he would like to find a house that's a little bigger.

_____

_____

_____

_____

_____

_____

_____

_____

H. List the things that you like and dislike about the place you currently live in.

喜歡   不喜歡

1. _____   1. _____

2. _____   2. _____

3. _____   3. _____

• • •   • • •

I. Based on the lists in the previous exercise, describe your ideal living quarters. (PRESENTATIONAL)

J. Storytelling (PRESENTATIONAL)

Write a story based on the four cartoons below. Make sure that your story has a beginning, middle and end. Also make sure that the transition from one picture to the next is smooth and logical.

18 LESSON 18 **Sports**
第十八課 運動

PART ONE **Dialogue I: My Gut Keeps Getting Bigger and Bigger!**

I. Listening Comprehension

A. Textbook Dialogue (True/False) (INTERPRETIVE)

( ) **1.** Wang Peng says he has been putting on weight.

( ) **2.** Gao Wenzhong wants to start exercising right away.

( ) **3.** Gao Wenzhong hasn't exercised in two years.

( ) **4.** Wang Peng suggests that Gao Wenzhong take up martial arts.

( ) **5.** Gao Wenzhong thinks playing basketball is too expensive.

B. Workbook Telephone Message (Multiple Choice) (INTERPRETIVE)

Bai Ying'ai called Gao Wenzhong, but he was not in, so she left him a message. Answer the following questions after you listen to the message.

( ) **1.** Bai Ying'ai called Gao Wenzhong to ask him to

    a. attend her birthday party.

    b. play tennis.

    c. have breakfast.

    d. meet her classmate.

( ) **2.** Bai Ying'ai suggests that Gao Wenzhong should

    a. buy a tennis racket.

    b. buy some tennis balls.

    c. hire a tennis coach.

    d. get a pair of tennis shoes.

( ) **3.** Who else may be there?

    a. Bai Ying'ai's father.

    b. Bai Ying'ai's classmate.

    c. Bai Ying'ai's pal Wang Peng.

    d. Bai Ying'ai's teacher.

( ) **4.** Bai Ying'ai thinks that Gao Wenzhong may not want to go because

    a. Gao Wenzhong feels tennis shoes are too expensive.

    b. Gao Wenzhong doesn't eat breakfast.

    c. Gao Wenzhong can't get up early.

    d. Gao Wenzhong isn't enthusiastic about playing sports.

C. Listening Rejoinder (INTERPERSONAL)

In this section, you will hear two speakers talking. After hearing the first speaker, select the best from the four possible responses given by the second speaker.

_____

II. Speaking Exercises

A. Answer the questions in Chinese based on the Textbook Dialogue. (INTERPRETIVE/PRESENTATIONAL)

1. According to Wang Peng, why has Gao Wenzhong gained weight?
2. How often and for how long does Wang Peng recommend Gao Wenzhong should exercise?
3. How long has it been since Gao Wenzhong exercised?
4. What sports does Wang Peng recommend?
5. What excuse does Gao Wenzhong give for disliking jogging?
6. Why does Wang Peng recommend swimming?
7. What is Wang Peng's conclusion?

B. Ask your partner if he/she exercises, how often, what kind of exercise he/she does, and why he/she likes that kind of exercise. (INTERPERSONAL)

III. Reading Comprehension (INTERPRETIVE)

A. Building Words

If you combine the *pǎo* in *pǎo bù* with the *chē* in *qìchē*, you have *pǎochē*, as seen in #1 below. Can you guess what the word *pǎochē* means? Complete this section by providing the characters, the *pinyin*, and the English equivalent of each new word formed this way. You may consult a dictionary if necessary.

		new word	*pinyin*	English
1.	"跑步"的"跑" + "汽車"的"車" → 跑+車 →		_____	_____	_____
2.	"上網"的"網" + "人民"的"民" → 網+民 →		_____	_____	_____
3.	"一把花"的"花" + "籃球"的"籃" → 花+籃 →		_____	_____	_____
4.	"游泳"的"泳" + "衣服"的"衣" → 泳+衣 →		_____	_____	_____
5.	"危險"的"危" + "樓下"的"樓" → 危+樓 →		_____	_____	_____

B. Read the following passage and answer the questions.

　　大明是小明的哥哥，他們都喜歡運動。大明每個星期打一次籃球，有時候還跟朋友一起去打網球。要是朋友都很忙，不能去打球，大明就自己一個人去跑步。小明跟大明不一樣，已經兩年沒有運動了，只喜歡看別人運動。他覺得球賽比什麼都好看，電視裏一有籃球比賽或者網球賽，小明就坐在沙發上看，有時候連飯都不想吃。大明今年三十五歲，但因為常常運動，身體好極了。小明今年只有二十五歲，可是越來越胖。大明小明兩個人在一起，不認識他們的人常說大明是弟弟，小明是哥哥。小明不懂為什麼他和哥哥都喜歡運動，可是身體沒有哥哥那麼好。

Questions (True/False)

( ) **1.** The older brother looks younger than the younger brother.
( ) **2.** Running is Daming's favorite kind of exercise.
( ) **3.** The last time Xiaoming exercised was two years ago.
( ) **4.** When there is a ball game on TV, Xiaoming doesn't want to watch anything else.
( ) **5.** Xiaoming has gained weight because he doesn't eat regularly.
( ) **6.** Both brothers love sports, but in very different ways.

C. Read the following passage and answer the questions.

哥哥：你最近常常生病，身體越來越糟糕，要想身體好，就得運動。運動不必多，做一種運動就夠了。

弟弟：一種運動就夠了？我做過好幾種運動，可是一點兒用都沒有。半年前我就開始打網球了。

哥哥：網球是一種很好的運動。你現在跟誰一起打？

弟弟：我五個月沒打網球了。我覺得游泳更有意思，所以打了兩次網球，就去游泳了。

哥哥：游泳也不錯。你現在在哪兒游泳？

弟弟：我四個月沒游泳了。我游了兩個多星期的泳，覺得還是打籃球方便，就開始打籃球了。

哥哥：你不說我也知道，你打了幾次籃球，覺得沒什麼意思，好幾個月沒打了，對不對？我現在才知道，你的身體為什麼這麼不好。

1. What was the older brother's initial advice to the younger brother on losing weight?

_____

2. What sports did the younger brother try recently?

_____

3. How long did the younger brother play tennis?

_____

4. When did the younger brother stop going swimming?

_____

5. Why do you think none of the sports worked for the younger brother?

_____

6. Why did the older brother change his estimate of the younger brother's chances of getting healthy?

_____

D. Answer the following question based on the TV guide provided.

BTV6
11:15 籃球風雲
13:15 奧運故事365
16:00 NBA 精彩回放
21:25 直播：天天體育

What time(s) can you definitely watch basketball programming?   _____

IV. Writing Exercises

A. Answer the following questions and explain your opinions.

1.   什麼運動很危險？

 _____

2. 什麼運動很簡單？

   → _____

3. 什麼運動很麻煩？

   → _____

4. 什麼運動得花很多時間？

   → _____

5. 什麼運動得花很多錢？

   → _____

B. Little Wang has been so busy studying this semester that he has neglected a lot of other things. State what he hasn't had time to do, and for how long, based on the illustrations given.

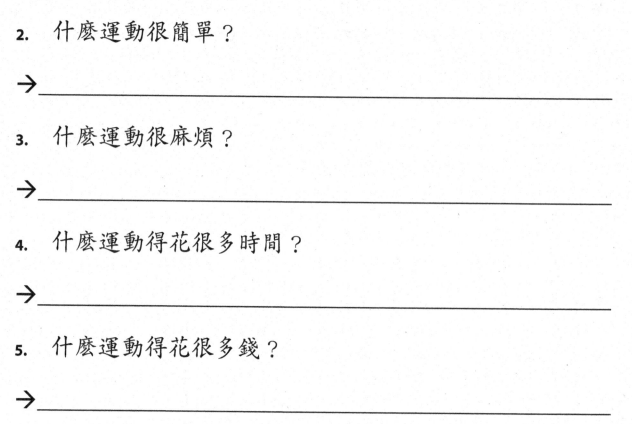

EXAMPLE: two months

→ 小王兩個月沒運動了。

1.   a week

   → _____

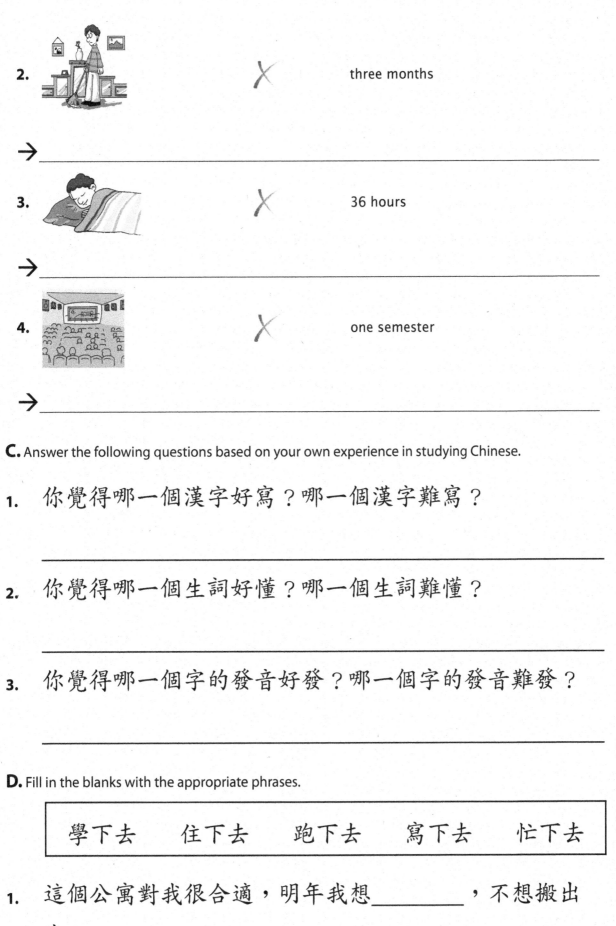

2.   ✗   three months

→ _____

3.   ✗   36 hours

→ _____

4.   ✗   one semester

→ _____

C. Answer the following questions based on your own experience in studying Chinese.

1. 你覺得哪一個漢字好寫？哪一個漢字難寫？

   _____

2. 你覺得哪一個生詞好懂？哪一個生詞難懂？

   _____

3. 你覺得哪一個字的發音好發？哪一個字的發音難發？

   _____

D. Fill in the blanks with the appropriate phrases.

學下去	住下去	跑下去	寫下去	忙下去

1. 這個公寓對我很合適，明年我想_____，不想搬出
   去。

2. 我寫日記寫了很多年了，還會_____。

3. 中文非常有意思，我下個學期一定_____。

4. 你最近忙得不能好好兒吃飯、睡覺，再這麼_____，
   一定會生病，休息幾天吧。

E. Translate the following into Chinese. (PRESENTATIONAL)

1. **A:** Why don't you like to swim? Are you afraid of water?

   _____

   B: Of course not. I feel it's too much trouble to go swimming.

   _____

2. **A:** You studied dancing for three years. Why didn't you continue?

   _____

   B: I was too tired, and I was not willing to continue.

   _____

   A: How long has it been since you danced?

   _____

   B: It's been more than six months.

   _____

3. I have studied Chinese for more than seven months. My teacher asked us to listen to the audio recordings for half an hour every day. But I haven't done so for more than a week. There's a test tomorrow. I'd better review thoroughly and hope that I will ace the test.

   _____

   _____

   _____

PART TWO — Dialogue II: Watching American Football

I. Listening Comprehension

A. Textbook Dialogue (True/False) (INTERPRETIVE)

( ) **1.** Wang Hong has watched soccer in the past.
( ) **2.** Wang Hong is not familiar with American football.
( ) **3.** Gao Xiaoyin's boyfriend loves to watch American football.
( ) **4.** Wang Hong is instantly hooked on American football.

B. Workbook Dialogue (True/False) (INTERPRETIVE)

( ) **1.** The woman doesn't believe that Gao Wenzhong went to play tennis.
( ) **2.** Gao Wenzhong may not like playing tennis much, but he likes his tennis partner.
( ) **3.** The man gives high marks to Gao Wenzhong's positive attitude.
( ) **4.** Gao Wenzhong gave up tennis after one lesson.
( ) **5.** The woman thinks that Gao Wenzhong may well succeed in losing weight.

C. Listening Rejoinder (INTERPERSONAL)

In this section, you will hear two speakers talking. After hearing the first speaker, select the best from the four possible responses given by the second speaker.

II. Speaking Exercises

A. Answer the questions in Chinese based on the Textbook Dialogue. (INTERPRETIVE/PRESENTATIONAL)

1. How much time did Wang Hong spend watching TV and why?
2. What kind of game did Gao Xiaoyin want to watch?
3. What two differences between American football and soccer did Gao Xiaoyin mention?
4. Why did Wang Hong want to switch the TV channel?
5. Do you think that Gao Xiaoyin's boyfriend likes to watch American football? Why or why not?

B. Ask your partner how often he/she watches TV and whether he/she watches sports on TV. If so, which sports does he/she watch? (INTERPERSONAL)

C. Tell your classmates whether you like to watch American football and explain the reasons why you like or dislike watching it. (PRESENTATIONAL)

III. Reading Comprehension (INTERPRETIVE)

A. Building Words

If you combine the *sài* in *bǐsài* with the *pǎo* in *pǎo bù*, you have *sàipǎo*, as seen in #1 below. Can you guess what the word *sàipǎo* means? Complete this section by providing the characters, the *pinyin*, and the English equivalent of each new word formed this way. You may consult a dictionary if necessary.

	new word	*pinyin*	English

1. "比賽"的"賽" + "跑步"的"跑"

   → 賽+跑 → _____ _____ _____

2. "比賽"的"賽" + "唱歌"的"歌"

   → 賽+歌 → _____ _____ _____

3. "水平"的"平" + "手"

   → 平+手 → _____ _____ _____

4. "天氣"的"氣" + "壓壞"的"壓"

   → 氣+壓 → _____ _____ _____

5. "運動"的"動" + "寵物"的"物"

   → 動+物 → _____ _____ _____

B. Read the following passage and answer the questions.

　　為了提高自己的中文水平，白先生每天下午開車到圖書館去看兩個多小時的中國電影。今天吃完午飯他想去圖書館，才想起來自己的汽車剛被表弟開回家去了。他打電話請表弟把車開回來，可是表弟的太太説，車讓他開到機場去了。白先生知道今天不能去圖書館了。

Questions (True/False)

( ) **1.** Mr. Bai is most likely a native Chinese speaker.

( ) **2.** Mr. Bai spends at least two hours in the library every day.

( ) **3.** Mr. Bai's home is not within walking distance of the library.

( ) **4.** Mr. Bai drove his cousin's car to the library yesterday.

( ) **5.** His cousin was not home when Mr. Bai called.

( ) **6.** Mr. Bai still plans on going to the library later this afternoon.

C. Read the passage and answer the questions.

　　張英和妹妹都喜歡打網球。張英每個星期六下午打兩個小時的球，然後回家吃晚飯。上個星期六她沒打，因為球拍被妹妹拿去了。妹妹那天要跟朋友打球，她覺得姐姐的球拍比她的好。今天又是星期六。張英告訴媽媽她晚上七點半才會回家吃晚飯，因為上個星期六她沒打球，所以今天要打四個小時的球。

1. Why didn't Zhang Ying play tennis last Saturday?

   _____

2. What did Zhang Ying's sister do last Saturday?

   _____

3. When do you think Zhang Ying will start playing tennis today?

   _____

4. Does Zhang Ying usually have dinner at 7:30 on Saturdays?

   _____

5. How much longer than usual will Zhang Ying play tennis today?

   _____

D. Read the passage and answer the questions.

高小音的男朋友很喜歡運動。他每天游一個小時的泳，每個星期打一次籃球。他没有踢過美式足球，可是美式足球是他最喜歡看的球賽。高小音剛從英國來美國的時候，不太懂美式足球，可是現在跟男朋友一樣，都愛看美式足球，電視上一有美式足球賽他們倆就連飯也忘了吃。

Questions (True/False)

(　) **1.** Gao Xiaoyin's boyfriend is a good swimmer, good basketball player, and good football player.

(　) **2.** Gao Xiaoyin's boyfriend exercises at least seven hours every week.

(　) **3.** Gao Xiaoyin was a football fan before she came to the United States.

(　) **4.** Gao Xiaoyin felt that her boyfriend's enthusiasm for football was contagious.

(　) **5.** Before watching a football game on TV, they usually have a meal in a restaurant.

E. Here's a daily TV guide for the sports channels. Do you see any soccer programs? If so, please circle them.

體育電視菜單　9月11日

0700 MLB美國職棒大聯盟： 　　　費城人對亞特蘭大勇士	2030 2003年世界花式撞球大師賽：NICK VAN 　　　DEN BERG對 FRANCISCO BUSTAMANTE
1000 (直播)MLB美國職棒大聯盟： 　　　舊金山巨人對亞歷桑納響尾蛇	2130 MLB美國職棒大聯盟： 　　　舊金山巨人對亞歷桑納響尾蛇
1300 足球:進球大匯串	0030 (首播) WWE HEAT
1330 英超指南	0130 第八屆冬季X GAMES － 趣味鏡頭
1400 (首播)2004年世界排球大獎賽： 　　　阿根廷對澳洲：第二場	0155 (直播) 2004/05年西班牙甲級足球聯 　　　賽：皇家馬德里對努曼西亞
1530 MLB美國職棒大聯盟： 　　　舊金山巨人對亞歷桑納響尾蛇	0400 亞洲賽車集錦
1830 (首播)ESPN趣味野外競賽	0430 (直播) 女子職業高爾夫

IV. Writing Exercises

A. Building Characters

Form a character by fitting the given components together as indicated. Then provide a word or phrase in which that character appears.

EXAMPLE: 左邊一個 "月" ，右邊一個 "土" 是 <u>"肚子"</u> 的
<u>"肚"</u> 。

1. 左邊一個 "月" ，右邊一個 "半天" 的 "半"
是＿＿＿＿＿＿ 的 ＿＿＿＿ 。

2. 左邊一個提手旁，右邊一個 "白色" 的 "白"
是＿＿＿＿＿＿ 的 ＿＿＿＿ 。

3. 左邊一個提手旁，右邊一個 "是"
是＿＿＿＿＿＿的 ＿＿＿＿ 。

4. 左邊一個足字旁，右邊一個 "容易" 的 "易"
是＿＿＿＿＿＿的 ＿＿＿＿ 。

5. 上邊一個 "音樂" 的 "音" ，下邊一個 "中心" 的
"心" 是＿＿＿＿＿＿的 ＿＿＿＿ 。

B. Answer the following questions based on your own workout routine.

1. 你喜歡什麼運動？

＿＿＿＿＿＿＿＿＿＿＿＿＿＿＿＿＿＿＿＿＿＿＿

2. 你常常去什麼地方運動？

＿＿＿＿＿＿＿＿＿＿＿＿＿＿＿＿＿＿＿＿＿＿＿

3. 你一個星期/一個月運動幾次？

_____

4. 你每次運動多長時間？

_____

5. 你多長時間沒運動了？

_____

C. Answer the following questions based on your own situation.

1. 你的中文老師平常坐著上課還是站著上課？

_____

2. 你常常坐著還是躺著聽音樂？

_____

3. 你覺得抱著球跑累不累？

_____

D. Take a look at the chart and summarize who did what for how long yesterday.

EXAMPLE:

李友昨天打掃房子打掃了兩個小時/鐘頭。

or   李友昨天打掃了兩個小時（的）房子。

1. _____

2. _____

3. _____

4. _____

5. _____

E. Describe the following situations based on the illustrations given.

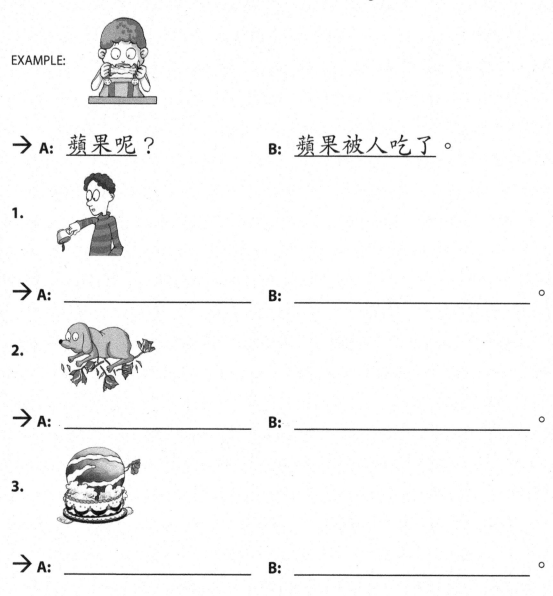

EXAMPLE:

→ A: 蘋果呢？   B: 蘋果被人吃了。

1.

→ A: _____   B: _____ 。

2.

→ A: _____   B: _____ 。

3.

→ A: _____   B: _____ 。

F. Translate the following into Chinese. (PRESENTATIONAL)

1. A: The weather is getting colder and colder. You'd better put on some more clothes. Otherwise, you may catch a cold.

_____

B: Don't worry. I am in great physical condition. I don't get sick easily.

_____

2. A: How come my tennis ball is not round any more?

_____

B: I am sorry. It got crushed by the sofa.

_____

3. A: Class, I have a fever. Today I have to give the lesson sitting down.

_____

B: Teacher, you should go home and rest.

_____

4. A: Old Wang, do you know how to send text messages?

_____

B: I don't. I don't even know how to e-mail.

_____

A: Old Wang, you don't even have a cell phone, right?

_____

B: Right!

_____

G. Design your own ideal weekly workout schedule, including types of exercise, locations, frequency, and duration of each workout. (PRESENTATIONAL)

H. Storytelling (PRESENTATIONAL)

Write a story based on the four cartoons below. Make sure that your story has a beginning, middle, and end. Also make sure that the transition from one picture to the next is smooth and logical.

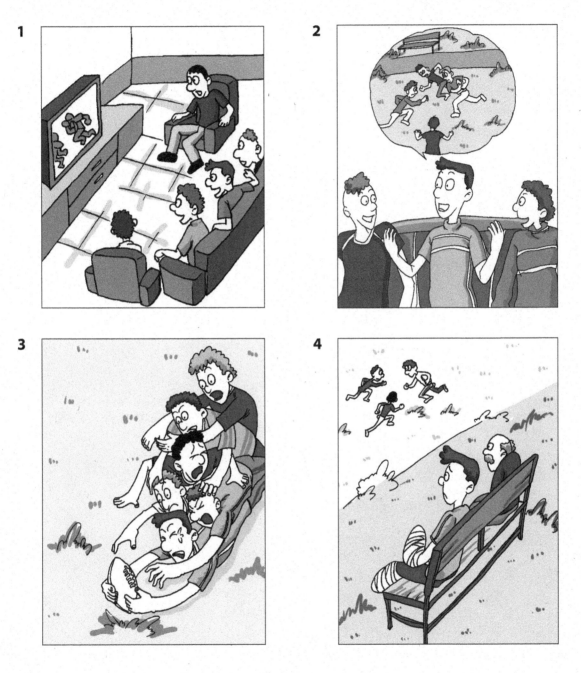

19

LESSON 19   Travel

第十九課 旅行

PART ONE   **Dialogue I: Traveling to Beijing**

I. Listening Comprehension

A. Textbook Dialogue (Multiple Choice) (INTERPRETIVE)

( ) **1.** What does Wang Peng plan to do during the summer break?

    a. apply for an internship
    b. visit his parents
    c. take summer classes
    d. get a part-time job

( ) **2.** At the beginning of the conversation, what summer plans did Li You have?

    a. nothing definite
    b. get a part-time job
    c. visit her parents
    d. take summer classes

( ) **3.** Li You seems to be especially interested in Beijing's many_____.

    a. good restaurants
    b. important libraries
    c. cultural centers
    d. interesting stores

( ) **4.** If Li You wanted to leave for Beijing today, she wouldn't have to worry about _____.

    a. her passport and airline ticket
    b. her passport and Chinese visa
    c. her tour guide and airline ticket
    d. her passport and tour guide

B. Workbook Dialogue (True/False) (INTERPRETIVE)

( ) **1.** The woman would like to go to Northern California because she wouldn't have to speak a foreign language.

( ) **2.** The woman doesn't like to fly, and she doesn't like hot weather.

( ) **3.** The man doesn't think much of Northern California, but the woman manages to persuade him of its charms.

( ) **4.** It seems that the woman has been to Northern California before.

C. Listening Rejoinder (INTERPERSONAL)

In this section, you will hear two speakers talking. After hearing the first speaker, select the best from the four possible responses given by the second speaker.

_____

II. Speaking Exercises

A. Answer the questions in Chinese based on the Textbook Dialogue. (INTERPRETIVE/PRESENTATIONAL)

1. What will Wang Peng's classmates do over the summer?
2. What is Wang Peng's plan for the summer?
3. What did Wang Peng say about Beijing?
4. Which cities in Asia has Li You visited before?
5. What does Li You need to do in order to travel to Beijing?

B. Ask your partner whether he/she plans to travel, work, study, or do something else during his/her summer vacation. (INTERPERSONAL)

C. Search online to find out how long it takes and how much it costs to obtain a tourist visa to China. Compare notes with your partner and report to the class. (PRESENTATIONAL)

III. Reading Comprehension (INTERPRETIVE)

A. Building Words

If you combine the *chūn* in *chūntiān* with the *jià* in *fàng jià*, you have *chūnjià*, as seen in #1 below. Can you guess what the word *chūnjià* means? Complete this section by providing the characters, the *pinyin*, and the English equivalent of each new word formed this way. You may consult a dictionary if necessary.

	new word	*pinyin*	English

1. "春天"的"春" + "放假"的"假"

   → 春+假 → _____ _____ _____

2. "放假"的"放" + "擔心"的"心"

   → 放+心 → _____ _____ _____

3. "養寵物"的"養" + "父母"的"父"

   → 養+父 → _____ _____ _____

4. "訂機票"的"訂" + "押金"的"金"

   → 訂+金 → _____ _____ _____

5. "報紙"的"報" + "旅行社"的"社"

   → 報+社 → _____ _____ _____

B. Read the following dialogue and answer the questions.

（還有三個星期學校就放假了。白英愛打算一放假就坐飛機回家去看爸爸媽媽，在家住三個星期，然後回學校。）

李友：　英愛，飛機票買好了嗎？

白英愛：買好了。比上次回家的機票便宜不少。

李友：　是嗎？你是在哪家旅行社買的？

白英愛：是高文中幫我在網上買的，他說在網上買又快、又方便、又便宜。

李友：　英愛，我覺得高文中很不錯。你一點兒都不喜歡他嗎？

白英愛：我也不知道我喜歡不喜歡他。昨天他聽說我放假要回家，就給我打手機說要開車送我去機場。

李友：　那你跟他說什麼？

白英愛：我說，要是他真的那麼喜歡開車，等我回來以後，我跟他一起開車去加州實習吧。

李友：　哎，英愛，那他一定高興得不得了。太好了！

Questions (True/False)

( ) **1.** Bai Ying'ai's summer break will last for only three weeks.
( ) **2.** Bai Ying'ai will leave as soon as the break starts.
( ) **3.** It was not hard for Bai Ying'ai to get an airline ticket at a good price this time.
( ) **4.** Gao Wenzhong will drive Bai Ying'ai to the airport.
( ) **5.** Bai Ying'ai probably does like Gao Wenzhong.

C. Read the following dialogue and answer the questions.

高小音：文中，學校要放假了，你有什麼打算？上暑期班還是再去我們圖書館打工？

高文中：不，我要和白英愛一起去加州的一家公司實習。

高小音：是嗎？

高文中：我和白英愛都沒去過，可是我看過不少加州的照片，真是漂亮得不得了。

高小音：我去過加州好幾次，就是在加州認識我男朋友的，所以我對加州的印象特別好。

高文中：是嗎？你想不想再去一次加州？當我們的導遊。

高小音：我當然想去，可是我工作太忙，也沒有假。

高文中：那我和白英愛在那兒多照幾張照片，用電子郵件
　　　　發給你吧。

Questions (True/False)

( ) **1.** Gao Wenzhong has never worked in Gao Xiaoyin's library.

( ) **2.** Gao Wenzhong has been to California before.

( ) **3.** California holds a special place in Gao Xiaoyin's heart.

( ) **4.** Gao Xiaoyin wishes that she could go with Gao Wenzhong.

( ) **5.** Gao Wenzhong's tour guide will help them take a lot of photos.

D. The following is a newspaper ad from a travel agency. Answer the questions based on the ad.

1. What city tour package is the ad promoting?_____

2. From which city will the tour depart?_____

3. What expenses are included in the tour package? Please list at least three.

_____

IV. Writing Exercises

A. Answer the following questions based on your own situation.

1. 學校幾月幾號開始放暑假？

   _____

2. 暑假放多長時間？

   _____

3. 暑假你打算做什麼？回家看父母、打工、出國旅行、
   在學校上暑期班，還是什麼都不做？

   _____

B. See if you can figure out the English names of the following airlines.

1. 美國航空公司   _____

2. 英國航空公司（英航）   _____

3. 加拿大航空公司（加航）   _____

4. 日本航空公司（日航）   _____

5. 西南航空公司   _____

6. 中國東方航空公司   _____

c.請把出國旅行以前得辦的事，得準備或者得帶的東西寫出來：

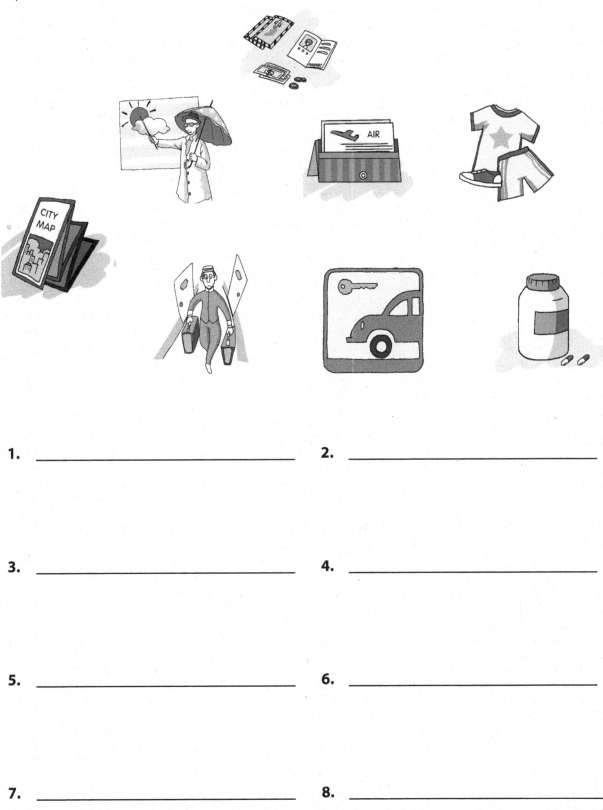

1. _____ 2. _____

3. _____ 4. _____

5. _____ 6. _____

7. _____ 8. _____

D. Fill in the blanks with the appropriate information.

EXAMPLE: Washington, D.C.

→Washington, D.C. 是美國的首都，也是美國的政治中心。

1. 北京→_____

2. 東京→_____

3. 紐約→_____

E. Translate the following into Chinese. (PRESENTATIONAL)

1. **A:** Have you ever heard of the Great Wall?

   _____

   B: Of course. The Great Wall is the most famous historic site in China. Everyone knows it. It's huge. Have you been to it?

   _____

   _____

   A: I haven't.

   _____

   B: I've been to the Great Wall many times. I'll take you there and be your tour guide.

   _____

2. How time flies! The summer break is around the corner. Some of my classmates are interning at different companies. Some are going home to work. I'll be traveling to Tokyo. Tokyo is the capital and the political and cultural center of Japan, with many famous historic sites. Good restaurants there are too many to count. I don't need a visa to go to Japan, and I have my airline ticket ready. I'm leaving tomorrow. See you next semester.

_____

_____

_____

_____

_____

F. Write an essay about which cities you have visited, and which of those cities gives you the best impression. Explain why you like that city. You may include information such as the weather, the people, the shopping, the tourist sites, whether the city is a political or cultural center, etc. Alternatively, pick a city you would like to visit in the future and write about why you have a good impression of that city as a travel destination. (PRESENTATIONAL)

歡迎刊登

旅遊廣告

What kind of ads are welcome here?

PART TWO Dialogue II: Planning an Itinerary

 ## I. Listening Comprehension

A. Textbook Dialogue (True/False) (INTERPRETIVE)

( ) **1.** Wang Peng and Li You will leave for Beijing in early June.

( ) **2.** Wang Peng and Li You plan to stay in Beijing for about a month.

( ) **3.** Wang Peng and Li You don't have any seat preferences for the flight to Beijing.

( ) **4.** Wang Peng asked for vegetarian meals for Li You and himself.

( ) **5.** Wang Peng decided to fly on Air China because the price is better.

B. Workbook Narrative (True/False) (INTERPRETIVE)

( ) **1.** Little Wang doesn't like flying because of safety reasons.

( ) **2.** The cabin temperature is never comfortable enough for Little Wang.

( ) **3.** Little Wang often gets an upset stomach from eating airline food.

( ) **4.** Little Wang often misses his connections because he spends too much time in airport restaurants.

( ) **5.** Little Wang prefers to travel by car.

C. Listening Rejoinder (INTERPERSONAL)

In this section, you will hear two speakers talking. After hearing the first speaker, select the best from the four possible responses given by the second speaker.

II. Speaking Exercises

A. Answer the questions in Chinese based on the Textbook Dialogue. (INTERPRETIVE/PRESENTATIONAL)

1. When does Wang Peng plan to go back to Beijing this summer?
2. What is his strategy for deciding which airline to fly on?
3. Why did Wang Peng choose to fly on Air China?
4. Did Wang Peng ask for aisle or window seats?
5. What else did Wang Peng request?

B. Do a role play with a partner. One of you is a traveler, and the other is a travel agent. The traveler calls the travel agent to inquire about ticket prices from where he/she lives to Beijing, Hong Kong, or Taipei. As the traveler, you should tell the agent about your departure and return dates, the airlines you are interested in, and your preferences for seating and meals. As the agent, you should give the passenger a few different options and try to come to an agreement about his/her travel plans. (INTERPERSONAL)

C. Tell your classmates about a recent trip, your favorite trip, or a trip you would like to take in the future. Remember to mention the purpose of the trip, the dates, your transportation arrangements, your travel companions, the length of the trip, and any enjoyable or frustrating aspects of the trip. (PRESENTATIONAL)

III. Reading Comprehension (INTERPRETIVE)

A. Building Words

If you combine the *dān* in *dānchéng* with the *hào* in *hàomǎ*, you have *dānhào*, as seen in #1 below. Can you guess what the word *dānhào* means? Complete this section by providing the characters, the *pinyin*, and the English equivalent of each new word formed this way. You may consult a dictionary if necessary.

		new word	*pinyin*	English
1.	"單程" 的 "單" + "號碼" 的 "號" → 單+號 →		_____	_____	_____
2.	"往返" 的 "返" + "航班" 的 "航" → 返+航 →		_____	_____	_____
3.	"直飛" 的 "飛" + "糖醋魚" 的 "魚" → 飛+魚 →		_____	_____	_____
4.	"轉機" 的 "轉" + "學校" 的 "學" → 轉+學 →		_____	_____	_____
5.	"快慢" 的 "快" + "素餐" 的 "餐" → 快+餐 →		_____	_____	_____

B. Read the passage and answer the questions.

　　小張和小藍是男女朋友。小張常常換工作，什麼工作錢多他就做什麼工作，哪兒的工作好他就去哪兒住。他十個月前從北京搬到香港，可是在香港只住了半年多，就在上海找到了一個錢更多的工作。小藍跟他不一樣，對錢沒有什麼興趣。哪個城市有文化她就喜歡哪個城市，所以她一直住在北京，哪兒也不想搬。小張說他每個星期都要坐飛機去北京看一次小藍，把錢都花在飛機票上了，希望以後能兩個星期飛一次。小藍說要是小張愛她，又不想花錢，很簡單，搬回北京。要不然，就再見。

Questions (True/False)

( ) **1.** Little Zhang has lived in three different cities in the past year.
( ) **2.** Little Zhang wants to experience life in different big cities.
( ) **3.** Little Zhang makes more money now than he did months ago.
( ) **4.** Little Lan is staying put because she has a well-paid job where she is.
( ) **5.** Little Zhang is not happy about spending money on airline tickets.
( ) **6.** Little Lan has given Little Zhang an ultimatum.

C. This is Teacher Gao's travel itinerary. Go over it and answer the questions in Chinese.

```
                                   Holiday Tours  假期旅遊


   12 JUN - WEDNESDAY
   UNITED        1547 COACH CLASS
   LV: SEATTLE           941A      NONSTOP                 CONFIRMED
   AR: SAN FRANCISCO    1145A
   SNACK-AUDIO                     SEAT-15D

   UNITED         857 COACH CLASS
   LV: SAN FRANCISCO     135P      NONSTOP                 CONFIRMED
   AR: SHANGHAI/PUDON    540P      ARRIVAL DATE-13 JUN
   LUNCH~LUNCH-MOVIE              SEAT-47C

   14 JUN - FRIDAY
   CHINA EASTER 5161 COACH CLASS
   LV: SHANGHAI/PUDON    345P      NONSTOP                 CONFIRMED
   AR: BEIJING           545P
   SNACK

   22 JUN - SATURDAY
   UNITED         852 COACH CLASS
   LV: BEIJING           925A      NONSTOP                 CONFIRMED
   AR: TOKYO/NARITA      150P
   LUNCH                          SEAT-34B

   UNITED         876 COACH CLASS
   LV: TOKYO/NARITA      455P      NONSTOP                 CONFIRMED
   AR: SEATTLE           930A
   DINNER-BREAKFAST-MOVIE         SEAT-35A
```

1. 你知道不知道高老師的飛機票是什麼時候訂的？

   _____

2. 你知道不知道飛機票是多少錢買的？

   _____

3. 高老師的飛機票是跟旅行社還是跟航空公司訂的？

   _____

4. 高老師哪一天走？從哪兒走？

   _____

5. 高老師到什麼地方去？

   _____

6. 高老師哪一天回美國？

   _____

7. 他回美國的航班號碼是多少？

   _____

8. 他買的是往返票還是單程票？

   _____

9. 高老師去中國的時候坐的是直飛的飛機嗎？

   _____

10. 位子訂好了嗎？

    _____

11. 旅行社的中文名字叫什麼？

    _____

D. Answer the following questions based on the menu.

午餐/晚餐

香港 – 北京

日本芥末蘋果雜菜沙拉

黑椒汁扣牛肉配白飯
或
紅酒燴豬柳配意大利麵

哈根達斯雪糕

麵包、牛油

誠意提供 太平洋咖啡

福茗堂茶莊
福建烏龍、福建特級香片

紅茶、日本綠茶

1.   This meal will be served on a flight between which two cities?_____

2.   Is this meal suitable for vegetarians? Why or why not?_____

3.   What beverages are available with the meal?_____

E. Look at the ad and answer the questions.

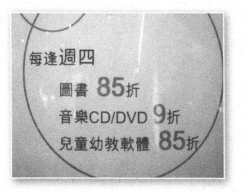

1.   Name two items that are on sale._____

2.   Which day of the week will customers get the discount?_____

F. Circle the baby bok choy. How much will you have to pay if the original price of the baby bok choy was $1?_____

What does 有機 mean?_____ (Hint: 有機 vegetables are more expensive than regular vegetables.)

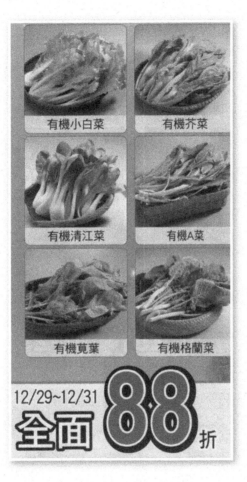

有機小白菜　　有機芥菜

有機清江菜　　有機A菜

有機莧葉　　有機格蘭菜

12/29~12/31　全面 8.8 折

IV. Writing Exercises

A. Building Characters

Form a character by fitting the given components together as indicated. Then provide a word or phrase in which that character appears.

EXAMPLE: 左邊一個 "土"，右邊一個 "成了好朋友" 的

"成" 是__"長城"__的__"城"__。

1. 上邊一個 "窗戶" 的 "戶"，下邊一個 "方便" 的

"方" 是_____的_____。

2. 左邊一個三點水，右邊一個"台北"的"台"

    是＿＿＿＿＿＿的＿＿＿。

3. 上邊一個"夕"，下邊一個"口"

    是＿＿＿＿＿＿的＿＿＿。

4. 左邊一個"汽車"的"車"，右邊一個"專業"的

    "專"是＿＿＿＿＿＿的＿＿＿。

5. 上邊一個"廣告"的"告"，下邊一個"非常"的

    "非"是＿＿＿＿＿＿的＿＿＿。

B. Search online to find out the population of the following cities, and express each city's population in Chinese.

EXAMPLE: 香港 (about 7,000,000)

→香港差不多有七百萬人。

1. 台北   →＿＿＿＿＿＿＿＿＿＿＿＿＿＿＿

2. 上海   →＿＿＿＿＿＿＿＿＿＿＿＿＿＿＿

3. 北京   →＿＿＿＿＿＿＿＿＿＿＿＿＿＿＿

4. 紐約   →＿＿＿＿＿＿＿＿＿＿＿＿＿＿＿

5. 東京   →＿＿＿＿＿＿＿＿＿＿＿＿＿＿＿

6. 我現在住的城市 →＿＿＿＿＿＿＿＿＿＿＿＿＿＿＿

C. First list the prices of the following items from two stores in Chinese. Then compare how much more or less expensive each item is at the two stores.

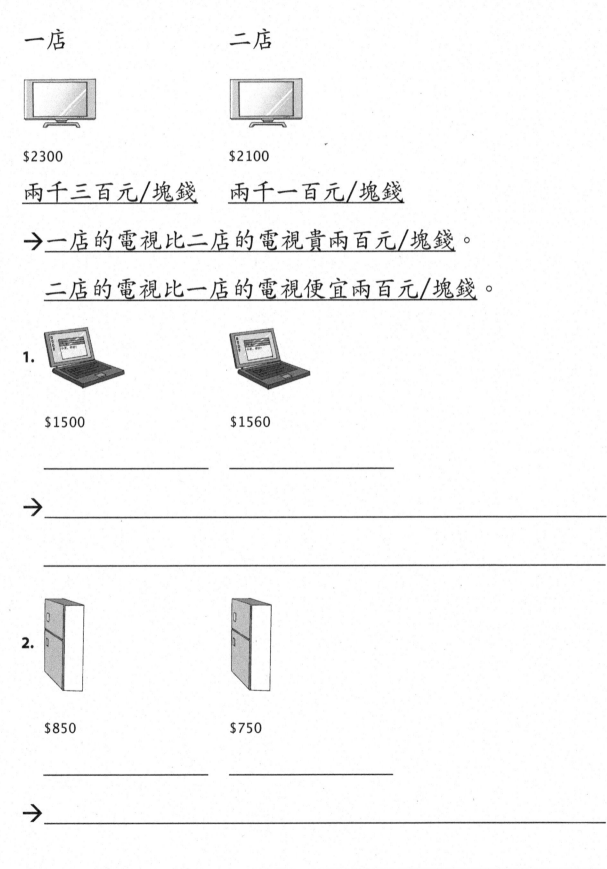

一店   二店

$2300 $2100

兩千三百元/塊錢   兩千一百元/塊錢

→一店的電視比二店的電視貴兩百元/塊錢。

二店的電視比一店的電視便宜兩百元/塊錢。

1.

$1500 $1560

_____   _____

→ _____

_____

2.

$850 $750

_____   _____

→ _____

_____

3.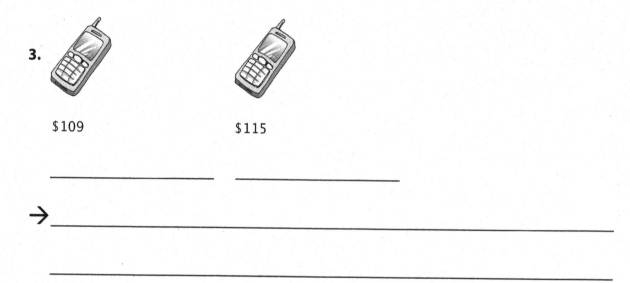

$109 $115

_____   _____

→ _____

_____

D. State what kind of discount the store is offering on the following items.

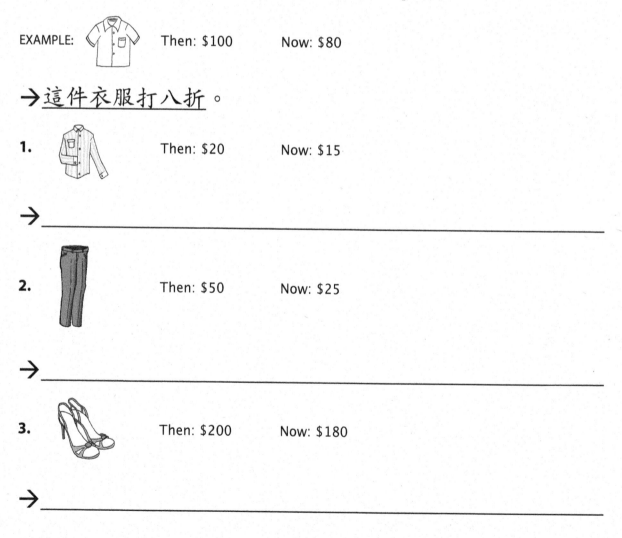

EXAMPLE: Then: $100   Now: $80

→這件衣服打八折。

1.   Then: $20   Now: $15

→ _____

2.   Then: $50   Now: $25

→ _____

3.   Then: $200   Now: $180

→ _____

E. Translate the following exchanges into Chinese. (PRESENTATIONAL)

1. A: Where would you like to sit?

_____

    B: I'll sit wherever you would like to.

_____

    A: Let's sit next to the window. What would you like to drink?

_____

    B: I'll have whatever you order.

_____

    A: What kind of dishes would you like to have?

_____

    B: I'll eat anything.

_____

2. A: I heard that airline tickets are on sale.

_____

    B: I'll go online and check right now.

_____

    A: Twenty percent off or thirty percent off?

_____

    B: The online ad says that if you buy a round-trip ticket, the second round-trip ticket will be fifty percent off.

_____

_____

    A: Then forget it.

_____

F. Imagine that you are a travel agent who just helped a customer plan her trip and book her airline tickets. Now you are going to go over the itinerary with the customer in Chinese, since she does not understand English. Be as detailed as possible, and include information such as when and where she is departing and returning, the route she is taking, how long each flight will take, the airlines she is taking, the flight numbers, whether the tickets are one-way or round-trip, whether the flights are nonstop, etc. (芝加哥 Zhījiāgē, 洛杉磯 Luòshānjī) (PRESENTATIONAL)

Southwest Airlines Air Itinerary						
Trip	Date	Day	Stops	Routing	Flight	Routing Details
Depart	Jul 15	Sat	N/S	MDW–LAX	971	Depart Chicago (MDW) at 1:05 PM Arrive in Los Angeles (LAX) at 3:20 PM
Return	Aug 04	Fri	N/S	LAX–MDW	723	Depart Los Angeles (LAX) at 10:20 AM Arrive in Chicago (MDW) at 4:15 PM

G. Storytelling

Write a story based on the four illustrations below. Make sure that your story has a beginning, middle and end. Also make sure that the transition from one picture to the next is smooth and logical. (PRESENTATIONAL)

酒 店　　機 票　　旅 遊　　商 旅

These are the services offered by a travel agency. Can you recognize some of the services?

LESSON 20 **At the Airport**
第二十課 在機場

PART ONE **Dialogue I: Checking In at the Airport**

I. Listening Comprehension

A. Textbook Dialogue (Multiple Choice) (INTERPRETIVE)

( ) **1.** How many people are seeing Wang Peng and Li You off at the airport?

     a. two
     b. three
     c. four
     d. five

( ) **2.** When did Wang Peng and Li You finish checking in?

     a. around 9:00
     b. around 10:00
     c. around 11:00
     d. around 12:00

( ) **3.** What will Bai Ying'ai be doing while Wang Peng and Li You are traveling?

     a. interning in New York
     b. going back home
     c. going to California with Gao Wenzhong
     d. joining Wang Peng and Li You in Beijing

( ) **4.** Wang Hong will be_____.

     a. all by herself
     b. with Gao Xiaoyin
     c. traveling with Gao Wenzhong and Bai Ying'ai
     d. going back to China in a few weeks

B. Workbook Narrative (True/False) (INTERPRETIVE)

( ) **1.** The speaker is likely an airline ground crew member.

( ) **2.** The flight is from Beijing to Shanghai.

( ) **3.** The plane will arrive at the destination at 3:00 pm.

( ) **4.** No snacks or beverages will be served because it is a short flight.

C. Listening Rejoinder (INTERPERSONAL)

In this section, you will hear two speakers talking. After hearing the first speaker, select the best from the four possible responses given by the second speaker.

_____

II. Speaking Exercises

A. Answer the questions in Chinese based on the Textbook Dialogue. (INTERPRETIVE/PRESENTATIONAL)

1. How many pieces of luggage did Wang Peng check?

2. Where should Wang Peng and Li You go to board the plane?

3. Why did Wang Hong sound worried?

4. What will Bai Ying'ai do this summer?

5. What did Li You say when she learned about Bai Ying'ai and Gao Wenzhong's summer plans?

6. What did Bai Ying'ai tell Wang Peng and Li You to do when they arrived in Beijing?

B. In Chinese, what do people usually say when they see their friends off? (PRESENTATIONAL)

C. Work with two or three people on a role play. Imagine you are at the local airport seeing your friend(s) off. Have a small talk right before the departure of your friend(s). (INTERPERSONAL)

III. Reading Comprehension (INTERPRETIVE)

A. Building Words

If you combine the *shū* in *shūdiàn* with *bāo*, you have *shūbāo*, as seen in #1 below. Can you guess what the word *shūbāo* means? Complete this section by providing the characters, the *pinyin*, and the English equivalent of each new word formed this way. You may consult a dictionary if necessary.

	new word	*pinyin*	English

1. "書店"的"書" + "包"

    → 書+包 → ＿＿＿＿＿ ＿＿＿＿＿ ＿＿＿＿＿

2. "超重"的"超" + "汽車"的"車"

    → 超+車 → ＿＿＿＿＿ ＿＿＿＿＿ ＿＿＿＿＿

3. "超重"的"超" + "高速公路"的"速"

    → 超+速 → ＿＿＿＿＿ ＿＿＿＿＿ ＿＿＿＿＿

4. "汽車"的"車" + "登機牌"的"牌"

    → 車+牌 → ＿＿＿＿＿ ＿＿＿＿＿ ＿＿＿＿＿

5. "出去"的"出" + "登機口"的"口"

    → 出+口 → ＿＿＿＿＿ ＿＿＿＿＿ ＿＿＿＿＿

B. Read the passage and answer the questions.

今天白英愛坐飛機回學校。她托運了一件大行李，然後帶著一個小包，護照和登機牌到九號登機口上飛機。上了飛機以後，白英愛剛在自己的位子上坐下，就聽到航空公司的一位女服務員跟大家說："這是去紐約的521號航班。要是您上錯了飛機，請您趕快下飛機。"她剛說完，坐在白英愛旁邊的兩位先生就說："不對！我們的航班是去紐約的，可是是531號！"女服務員聽了以後，就和另外一位服務員一起到飛機的前邊去了。五分鐘以後，她才回來對大家說："真對不起，你們是對的，這是531號航班。我們上錯飛機了。"

Questions (True/False)

( ) **1.** Bai Ying'ai had two pieces of baggage.
( ) **2.** Bai Ying'ai went to the wrong boarding gate.
( ) **3.** The men sitting next to Bai Ying'ai realized that they had boarded the wrong airplane.
( ) **4.** Both Flight 521 and Flight 531 were bound for New York.
( ) **5.** We can assume that Bai Ying'ai will not see that attendant during her flight.

C. Read the dialogue and answer the questions. (True/False)

高文中：英愛！

白英愛：文中！等了很久吧？飛機一個小時以前就到了，可是我等托運的行李等了半天了還沒等到。

高文中：真的？航空公司一定是把你的行李放錯飛機了。別擔心，他們會找到的。

白英愛：他們告訴我行李到了會給我打電話，要我等他們的電話。還好，我的信用卡、護照、錢，都在這個小包裹，要不然就麻煩了。下一班飛機是兩點半到，我想我的包一定在那個飛機上。我們還得等一個多小時。

高文中：那我們找個地方喝點咖啡吧。你知道嗎，李友後天要跟王朋一起去北京。

白英愛：是嗎？那我們後天可以去送他們。對了，我還沒
　　　　告訴李友我們要去加州，她可能以為我要去紐約
　　　　實習呢。

……

（航空公司的電話）：白英愛小姐嗎？非常對不起，我們剛
　　　　　　　　　　查到您托運的行李，您的行李現在正
　　　　　　　　　　在去東京的飛機上…

( ) 1. 白英愛的航班早到了一個小時。

( ) 2. 白英愛花了兩個半小時找她的行李，可是沒有
　　　　找到。

( ) 3. 高文中覺得白英愛的行李在別的飛機上。

( ) 4. 白英愛很擔心她托運的包，因為她的護照在那個
　　　　包裏。

( ) 5. 白英愛早就知道李友要和王朋一起去北京。

( ) 6. 李友還不知道白英愛最新的暑假計劃。

( ) 7. 白英愛一個多小時以後能拿到她托運的行李。

D. The following is a notice posted in an airport. Will it help people locate their luggage, airlines, or boarding gates?

_____

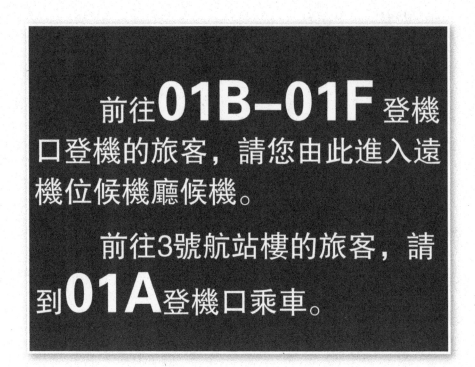

前往**01B-01F**登機口登機的旅客，請您由此進入遠機位候機廳候機。

前往3號航站樓的旅客，請到**01A**登機口乘車。

IV. Writing Exercises

A. Fill in the blanks with either 的, 得, or 地.

　　暑假快到了，大家都高高興興＿＿＿準備放假，有的人打算去旅行，有的人打算去實習。但也有的人什麼事都不想做，只想好好兒＿＿＿在家休息休息。

　　希望每個人＿＿＿暑假都過＿＿＿很好，下個學期再見。

B. Fill in the blanks with either 的時候 or 以後.

1. 生病＿＿＿＿＿＿＿＿，別亂跑，得在家休息。

2. 父母死了＿＿＿＿＿＿＿＿，都是大哥在照顧我們。

3. 開車＿＿＿＿＿＿＿＿，別打手機，太危險了。

4. 行李超重＿＿＿＿＿＿＿得多付錢。

5. 簽證辦好＿＿＿＿＿＿＿，就可以訂機票了。

C. Translate the following exchanges into Chinese. (PRESENTATIONAL)

1. **A:** Be careful. This place is dangerous. Don't run around.

   _____

   B: Don't worry. I'm sitting right here.

   _____

2. **A:** Don't forget to send me an e-mail when you get to Tokyo.

   _____

   B: OK... Don't cry. I'll be back in a month. Study hard at school.

   _____

   A: OK. Goodbye. Have fun.

   _____

D. Let's plan a trip to China. Choose two cities in China that you would like to visit. First explain why you're interested in these two cities, and then arrange your route from your current location. Search online for information about the cities, airfares, and hotel accommodations, and put together a travel itinerary. Your travel itinerary needs to include all the information on the flights, the airlines, the airfares, the time it will take to get to each destination and the time you plan to spend there, things you need to take care of before you depart, things you need to take with you on the trip, and your transportation to and from the airports. Don't forget to keep an eye on your budget. (PRESENTATIONAL)

E. Your friend from China is planning to travel within the United States and needs your help to understand the airline's rule. Use the information below to explain to your friend all the rules about luggage on this particular airline.

(pound: 磅, bàng) (PRESENTATIONAL)

Domestic Free Luggage Allowance

Each ticketed passenger traveling domestically is allowed one piece of checked luggage and one piece of carry-on luggage plus a purse or briefcase or laptop case. All checked and carry-on luggage is subject to the following limitations:

Checked Luggage

The Airline will accept checked luggage up to a maximum weight of 50 pounds (23kg). Luggage weighing between 50 and 70 pounds (23-32kg) will be assessed $25 USD per piece and luggage weighing between 70 and 100 pounds (32-46kg) will be assessed $50 USD per piece. Luggage weighing over 100 pounds (46kg) will not be accepted as checked luggage.

Carry-On Luggage

Each person is allowed to carry onboard the aircraft one piece of luggage. This piece of luggage must not exceed 40 pounds. In addition to this one piece of carry-on luggage, customers may also carry onboard a purse or briefcase or laptop computer. In addition, each passenger may carry a coat, umbrella, or other "special" items.

航空公司	班次	行李轉盤
Airlines	Flight No.	Carousel No.
美航	AA 7969	

班次＝班機＝航班

PART TWO   Dialogue II: Arriving in Beijing

I. Listening Comprehension

A. Textbook Dialogue (True/False) (INTERPRETIVE)

( ) **1.** Wang Peng's grandparents are waiting in the car outside the airport terminal.

( ) **2.** Wang Peng's parents are impressed with Li You's Chinese.

( ) **3.** Wang Peng has lost some weight due to his busy schedule.

( ) **4.** Wang Peng's parents plan to take Wang Peng and Li You directly home.

B. Workbook Narrative (True/False) (INTERPRETIVE)

Li You called her father from Beijing. Choose the best answers to the questions after listening to the message she left for him.

( ) **1.** Where is Li You?

    a. in a roast duck restaurant
    b. at the airport terminal
    c. at Wang Peng's parents' apartment
    d. in the car leaving the airport

( ) **2.** Li You promises to_____.

    a. call her dad again tomorrow
    b. catch up on her sleep
    c. buy a cell phone for her father
    d. buy some DVDs for her father

( ) **3.** Li You is_____.

    a. very tired
    b. homesick already
    c. impressed with the Beijing airport
    d. very impatient

( ) **4.** Li You is calling from_____.

    a. Wang Peng's cell phone
    b. Wang Peng's dad's cell phone
    c. Wang Peng's mom's cell phone
    d. her own cell phone

C. Listening Rejoinder (INTERPERSONAL)

In this section, you will hear two speakers talking. After hearing the first speaker, select the best from the four possible responses given by the second speaker.

_____

II. Speaking Exercises

A. Answer the questions in Chinese based on the Textbook Dialogue. (INTERPRETIVE/PRESENTATIONAL)

1. How did Li You address Wang Peng's parents?
2. How did Li You account for her Chinese language skills?
3. Wang Peng's mother thought that Wang Peng had lost some weight. What did she think was the reason?
4. What did Wang Peng say about how Wang Hong was doing in the United States?
5. Where were Wang Peng's grandparents?

B. What would you say to someone who compliments you on your Chinese? (PRESENTATIONAL)

C. Do a role play with two classmates. You are traveling with a Chinese friend and meeting his/her parent for the first time at an airport in China or Taiwan. Make up a conversation for the meeting. Address your host parent appropriately, and express your feelings about your flight. The Chinese friend should make sure to introduce everyone. The parent should ask you about the trip, what you would like to do on your visit, etc. (INTERPERSONAL)

III. Reading Comprehension (INTERPRETIVE)

A. Building Words

If you combine the *kǎo* in *kǎoyā* with the *ròu* in *niúròu*, you have *kǎo ròu*, as seen in #1 below. Can you guess what the word *kǎo ròu* means? Complete this section by providing the characters, the *pinyin*, and the English equivalent of each new word formed this way. You may consult a dictionary if necessary.

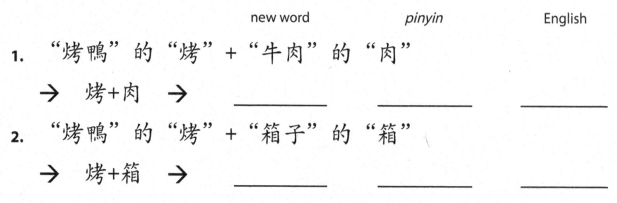

		new word	*pinyin*	English
1.	"烤鸭" 的 "烤" + "牛肉" 的 "肉" → 烤+肉 →		_____	_____	_____
2.	"烤鸭" 的 "烤" + "箱子" 的 "箱" → 烤+箱 →		_____	_____	_____

3. "烤鴨" 的 "鴨" + "蛋糕" 的 "蛋"

→ 鴨+蛋 → _____ _____ _____

4. "一塊錢" 的 "錢" + "包"

→ 錢+包 → _____ _____ _____

5. "海" + "托運" 的 "運"

→ 海+運 → _____ _____ _____

B. Read the passage and answer the questions.

　　王朋的妹妹王紅來美國找王朋的時候，她的爸爸、媽媽、爺爺和奶奶都到機場去送她。因為王紅的行李太多了，她爸爸的汽車放不下，所以爸爸跟媽媽開他們自己的車，王紅跟爺爺奶奶坐出租汽車去機場。因為這是王紅第一次出國，所以爸爸媽媽都很擔心，一直告訴她到美國以後要好好照顧自己。媽媽要王紅一到美國就讓哥哥給家裏打電話。王紅知道哥哥在美國一年了，有很多朋友，他們會照顧她的。她真不懂爸爸媽媽為什麼這麼擔心。

Questions (True/False)

( ) 1. 王紅去美國的時候不是坐爸爸的汽車去機場的。

( ) 3. 王紅去美國以前去過一次日本。

( ) 4. 王朋比王紅早一年去美國。

( ) 5. 王紅到美國以後就會打電話給爸爸媽媽。

( ) 6. 王紅出國，爸爸媽媽比王紅自己更擔心。

C. Read the passage and answer the questions.

王紅在高小音家住了三個月了，英文水平提高了不少。王紅說都是因為小音教得好，可是小音說是因為王紅聰明。為了謝謝小音照顧自己，王紅計劃秋天請小音跟她一起去北京，帶小音看看北京的名勝古蹟，當小音的導遊，還要請她吃北京烤鴨。為了準備去中國，小音這幾天每天都跟王紅說中文，希望自己中文越來越好，秋天去中國什麼都聽得懂，什麼都會說。

Questions (True/False)

( ) **1.** Wang Hong is quite modest about her English studies.

( ) **2.** Gao Xiaoyin is not satisfied with Wang Hong's English progress.

( ) **3.** Wang Hong wants to go back to Beijing in the fall because she's homesick.

( ) **4.** Wang Hong plans to hire a tour guide for Gao Xiaoyin.

( ) **5.** Gao Xiaoyin thinks her own Chinese is perfect.

D. Give the *pinyin* of the sentence seen here.

IV. Writing Exercises

A. Building Characters

Form a character by fitting the given components together as indicated. Then provide a word or phrase in which that character appears.

EXAMPLE: 左邊一個"力氣"的"力"，右邊一個"登機口"

的"口"是<u>"加州"</u>的<u>"加"</u>。

1. 上邊一個"木"，下邊一個"子"是＿＿＿＿＿＿

   的＿＿＿＿。

2. 左邊一個足字旁，右邊一個"包"是＿＿＿＿＿＿

   的＿＿＿＿。

3. 左邊一個人字旁，右邊一個"牛肉"的"牛"

   是＿＿＿＿＿＿的＿＿＿＿。

4. 上邊一個"田"，下邊一個"糸"

   是＿＿＿＿＿＿的＿＿＿＿。

5. 左邊一個"火"，右邊一個"考試"的"考"

   是＿＿＿＿＿＿的＿＿＿＿。

B. Answer the following questions. (PRESENTATIONAL)

1. 要是在機場或者車站送人，你會說些什麼話？

   ＿＿＿＿＿＿＿＿＿＿＿＿＿＿＿＿＿＿＿＿＿＿

   ＿＿＿＿＿＿＿＿＿＿＿＿＿＿＿＿＿＿＿＿＿＿

   ＿＿＿＿＿＿＿＿＿＿＿＿＿＿＿＿＿＿＿＿＿＿

2. 要是在機場或者車站接人，你會説些什麼話？

_____

_____

_____

C. Translate the following into Chinese. (PRESENTATIONAL)

1. A: You've worked for more than ten hours. You must be exhausted.

_____

B: I'm all right.

_____

A: You haven't had any food for eight hours. You must be starving.

_____

B: I'm OK.

2. A: I eat whatever you eat and drink whatever you drink. How come I'm getting fatter and fatter and you're getting thinner and thinner?

_____

B: I exercise two or three times a week. How about you? You haven't exercised for two years.

_____

3. Wang Peng emailed Wang Hong from Beijing. See if you can translate his email.

Sister:

We arrived in Beijing yesterday afternoon. We waited a long time for our checked luggage. Mom and Dad came to the airport to pick us up. Li You and I felt all right. We weren't too tired. As soon as we got out of the airport, we headed straight for the Peking duck restaurant for dinner. When we arrived at the restaurant, Grandma and Grandpa were already there. I hadn't had Peking duck for a long time, and enjoyed the food very much. Li You is a vegetarian, so she didn't have duck, and only had some vegetable dumplings. She ate faster than Grandma and Grandpa, and after she finished her food, she said in Chinese to Grandma and Grandpa: "Take time with the food." I think Grandma and Grandpa were happy after hearing that.

Your brother

_____

_____

_____

_____

_____

_____

_____

_____

D. Use the pictures to help you describe what people normally do: 1) one month before traveling overseas, 2) on the night before flying out, and 3) on the day of traveling. (PRESENTATIONAL)

1. _____

2. _____

3. _____

E. Pick a tourist/historical site in Beijing or another major Chinese-speaking city that you would like to visit. Search online for information on the site. Write a simple tourist pamphlet, including information on where it is located (east, south, west, or north of the city), how far it is from the airport, what transportation people can use to get there, why it is famous, etc. Don't forget to provide the pinyin and the characters for the name of the site. (PRESENTATIONAL)

F. Family Tree

Draw your family tree and list your family members and close relatives in Chinese. Use Grammar 4 in the textbook as a reference to complete the tree. (PRESENTATIONAL)

父親   母親

我

G. Storytelling (PRESENTATIONAL)

Write a story based on the four cartoons below. Make sure that your story has a beginning, middle and end. Also make sure that the transition from one picture to the next is smooth and logical.

I. How do you say these words/phrases?

Write down their correct pronunciation and tones in *pinyin*, and use a tape recorder or computer to record them. Hand in the recording to your teacher if asked.

1. 我們倆　我們兩個 ＿＿＿＿＿＿ ＿＿＿＿＿＿

2. 出租　　廚房　　叔叔 ＿＿＿＿＿ ＿＿＿＿＿ ＿＿＿＿＿

3. 傢具　　公寓　　旅行 ＿＿＿＿＿ ＿＿＿＿＿ ＿＿＿＿＿

4. 不准　　不瘦　　難受 ＿＿＿＿＿ ＿＿＿＿＿ ＿＿＿＿＿

5. 導遊　　游泳 ＿＿＿＿＿ ＿＿＿＿＿

6. 書架　　暑假 ＿＿＿＿＿ ＿＿＿＿＿

II. Group the characters according to their radicals, and provide the meaning of each radical.

Radical	Meaning of the Radical (English)	Characters
1. _____	_____	_____
2. _____	_____	_____
3. _____	_____	_____
4. _____	_____	_____
5. _____	_____	_____
6. _____	_____	_____

III. VO or Not

Among the verbs below, distinguish those that are VO compounds from those that are not.

打掃   整理   旅行   做飯   走路   游泳

跑步   放假   實習   打工   轉機   托運

VO Compounds: _____

not VO Compounds: _____

IV. Have You Seen that Character Before?

Circle the character shared by the words in each group. Write down the *pinyin* for the character in common, and define the character's original meaning.

			pinyin	meaning
1. 天氣	力氣	客氣	_____	_____
2. 一定	一言為定		_____	_____
3. 時間	房間	衛生間	_____	_____
4. 房間	廚房	房租	_____	_____

5. 預報　　報紙 _____ _____

6. 最近　　附近 _____ _____

7. 分鐘　　鐘頭 _____ _____

8. 教室　　臥室　　辦公室 _____ _____

9. 請客　　客氣　　客廳 _____ _____

10. 餐廳　　客廳 _____ _____

11. 暑期班　暑假 _____ _____

12. 禮物　　寵物 _____ _____

13. 發音　　發燒　　發短信 _____ _____

14. 平常　　水平　　平安 _____ _____

15. 平安　　安靜 _____ _____

16. 網上　　網球 _____ _____

17. 保險　　危險 _____ _____

18. 高興　　興趣 _____ _____

19. 名字　　有名　　名勝古蹟 _____ _____

20. 寒假　　暑假　　放假 _____ _____

21. 辦法　　怎麼辦　　辦公室 _____ _____

22. 長城　　城市　　中國城 _____ _____

23. 簡單　　單程 _____ _____

24. 告訴　　廣告 _____ _____

25. 走路　　走道 _____ _____

26. 運動　　托運 _____ _____

27. 喜歡　　歡迎 _____ _____

28. 起床　　起飛　　　　　　　　　＿＿＿＿＿　　＿＿＿＿＿

29. 公司　　公寓　　　　公園　　　　公共汽車　　高速公路

　　　　　　　　　　　　　　　　　　＿＿＿＿＿　　＿＿＿＿＿

30. 學習　　練習　　　　預習　　　　復習　　　　實習

　　　　　　　　　　　　　　　　　　＿＿＿＿＿　　＿＿＿＿＿

V. Getting to Know You

Put your Chinese to use. Interview one of your classmates to find out more about him/her. After a brief Q & A session, jot down and organize the information you have gathered, and then present an oral or written report to introduce your classmate to others. (INTERPERSONAL/PRESENTATIONAL)

A: Are you a sports fan?

1. 你對什麼運動有興趣？

2. 你對什麼球賽有興趣？

3. 你平常運動嗎？

    ✓ a. 你每個星期運動幾次？每次運動多長時間？

    ✗ b. 你多長時間沒運動了？

4. 你覺得什麼運動最簡單？為什麼？

5. 你覺得什麼運動最麻煩？為什麼？

6. 你覺得什麼運動最危險？為什麼？

B: Should I move or should I stay?

1. 你住的地方是宿舍、公寓、還是房子？住得下三個人嗎？

2. 你住的地方幾房幾廳？有沒有自己的廚房、衛生間？

3. 你住的地方帶不帶傢具？有什麼傢具？

4. 你覺得你的房間乾淨嗎？你常常整理房間嗎？

5. 你每個月打掃幾次房子？

6. 這個地方對你合適嗎？為什麼？

7. 你打算住下去還是搬出去？為什麼？

C. Do you like to travel?

1. 你去過哪些城市／國家？

2. 你對哪一個城市／國家的印象最好／最糟糕？

3. 你是什麼時候去的？怎麼去的？

4. 你在那兒玩兒了多長時間？

5. 你還會再去一次嗎？

6. 如果你有錢、有時間，你希望能到什麼地方去旅行？

7. 要是坐飛機，你怎麼訂票？你跟旅行社、航空公司訂機票，還是上網訂機票？

VI. Beijing vs. New York City

Both Beijing and New York City are big cities. Search online and find out more about the two cities. Compare the two, and see how similar or different they are. You can take on all six tasks or choose just a few. (INTERPRETIVE/PRESENTATIONAL)

1. Weather

Check the weather forecast for tomorrow for the two cities. Compare which city will be warmer or colder and whether it's supposed to rain tomorrow.

2. Population

List the population of the two cities. Then compare which city has more people.

3. Transportation

Find out what means of public transportation are available in each city and compare which public transportation system is more convenient. Figure out where the international airports are located in relation to the downtown area, and how to get to them.

4. Shopping

List today's currency exchange rate for U.S. dollars and RMB. Find out how much a watermelon, a refrigerator, and a basketball would cost in a local store in each city. Compare the prices between the two cities.

5. Housing

List today's currency exchange rate for U.S. dollars and RMB. Find out how much it would cost to rent an apartment with two bedrooms and one bathroom in each city.

6. Traveling

Find one US airline and one Chinese airline that provide flight service between the two cities. Describe the route they take, the times the flights depart, the flight time, the airfares, how many meals they serve onboard, etc. Compare the two options, and figure out which airline has better ticket prices, a shorter flight time, and better service.